Orthodox Christian
Bible Commentary

# 2 CORINTHIANS

By His Eminence Metropolitan Youssef

ST MARY & MOSES ABBEY PRESS

# ⊰ *Contents* ⊱

# St. Paul's Second Epistle to the Corinthians

**AUTHOR: St. Paul.** We read in verse one: "Paul, an apostle of Jesus Christ by the will of God, and Timothy our brother"; the author is clearly St. Paul with the accompaniment of St. Timothy—together.

**PLACE: Macedonia.** While St. Paul was in Macedonia, en route for another visit to Corinth, he wrote this letter to the Corinthians. This would be during his third missionary journey, of which St. Luke says very little (Acts 20:1-2)

**TIME: Fall A.D. 57.** We know that St. Paul made three missionary trips. He wrote this letter while in Macedonia, during his third missionary trip. Actually, St. Luke wrote in the Book of Acts very briefly about St. Paul's stay and dictation of this letter in Macedonia.

We read in Acts, Chapter 20:1–2, "After the uproar had ceased, Paul called the disciples to himself, embraced them and departed to Macedonia. Now when he had gone over that region and encouraged them with many words, he came to Greece."

During his stay in Macedonia, mentioned in Acts 20, St. Paul wrote the Second Epistle to the Corinthians.

The time of writing is most likely during the fall of the year A.D. 57, which is actually just a few months after writing the first letter. The first letter was written in the spring, perhaps around April because he had told them he wanted to spend Pentecost in Jerusalem. If the first letter was written in the spring, and this one was written in the fall, then it is perhaps only 5 months later.

## BACKGROUND

Who carried this Letter to Corinth? Titus, his disciple, carried the letter to

Corinth, as we read in Chapter 8:16-22:

> But thanks be to God who puts the same earnest care for you into the heart of Titus. For he not only accepted the exhortation, but being more diligent, he went to you of his own accord. And we have sent with him the brother whose praise is in the gospel throughout all the churches, and not only that, but who was also chosen by the churches to travel with us with this gift, which is administered by us to the glory of the Lord Himself and to show your ready mind, avoiding this: that anyone should blame us in this lavish gift which is administered by us— providing honorable things, not only in the sight of the Lord, but also in the sight of men. And we have sent with them our brother whom we have often proved diligent in many things, but now much more diligent, because of the great confidence which we have in you.

St. Paul is saying he is sending Titus with two other brethren, "therefore show to them, and before the churches, the proof of your love and of our boasting on your behalf" (1 Cor 1:24).

St. Paul sent this letter, through Titus mainly, with other brethren.

## **PURPOSE**

Why did St. Paul write this letter, only a few months after writing the first letter? If you recall, Corinth had many problems, and St. Paul addresses all these problems in the first letter. Actually, he rebuked them over many issues. One of the issues being the adultery that occurred in the church.

The church in Corinth began in A.D. 52; St. Paul having visited them in his second missionary trip, stayed a year-and-half with them. Perhaps, this was the first time for him to stay such a long time in one city. Because he had rebuked them, he now wanted to see the reaction to his letter—whether they had repented or not.

As a father, he wanted to make sure that this rebuke was received positively and that it actually encouraged them to repent. We can read about the first visit in Acts 18:1–18. After he left Corinth following the first visit, he received a report from Titus, informing him of how they received the first Letter, of their repentance, and of how they benefited from his rebuke – as we read in 2 Corinthians Chapter 2:12 and Chapter 7:5–9.

The sequence was as follows: St. Paul went to Corinth, spent a year-and-half there, and after learning some negative news about Corinth, he wrote the letter, sending it there with Titus, who brought back a good report of how they received the letter and repented. St. Paul sent the other letter to encourage them and to show them that he was grateful for their repentance; once again, this letter was sent with Titus.

Titus's report was encouraging, but another problem began appearing in Corinth. The problems mentioned in the first Letter were now taken care of, but another problem materialized: people began to cast doubts on the apostleship of St. Paul. They started saying that he was not a real apostle because he was not one of the twelve.

St. Paul began his introduction, "Paul, a bondservant of Jesus Christ," but in this chapter, he did not describe himself as a bondservant of Jesus Christ, rather, here he said, "Paul, an apostle of Jesus Christ by the will of God." He is saying, "My apostleship is true. It is by the will of God, not by the will of men."

Why was it very important for St. Paul to defend his apostleship? Because if his apostleship were not defended, this would mean that all the churches that he had established were not really churches, and the ordination of all the bishops and priests that he ordained would be illegitimate. That is why St. Paul wanted to defend his apostleship— for the sake of the churches that he established, and the clergy he ordained.

This doubt regarding his apostleship was planted by teachers who came from a Jewish background—we call them "Judaizing teachers,"—who said that St. Paul attacked salvation by the Law only, without the grace of God. That is why these people attempted to undermine St. Paul's teaching about the Law, and how a person will be saved by the Law, without the grace of God.

They cast doubts on his integrity. They said that St. Paul made promises but does not keep them. Because he changed his plans to visit Corinth, they said that he is not a man of his word; his "yes" can be no, and his "no" can be yes.

They also attacked his style of writing and his speaking ability. They said that he usually speaks in ambiguous ways, to confuse people and avoid being held accountable. Usually, when people speak ambiguously, you cannot hold them accountable because they say words that carry so many different meanings; such that if you want to confront them saying, "You said so," they can say, "No, I did not mean it that way."

Further, they attacked him for his unwillingness to accept support from the church at Corinth, as we can see from Chapter 11:7–9, and Chapter 12:13.

So they attacked him, they attacked his apostleship, they attacked his promises, his speaking ability and style of writing, and also his unwillingness to accept support from the church at Corinth.

Reasons why St. Paul wrote this letter: some people in Corinth still had not repented from their ungodly behavior, especially sexual immorality and licentiousness. St. Paul actually rebuked them and tried to lead them to repentance, as we read in Chapter 12:20 & 21.

St. Paul hoped that by writing before his visit, he could get all the necessary rebuke out of the way. Meaning that St. Paul wanted his visit to be a blessed, pleasant visit. That is a second reason why he wrote this letter: if there is any rebuke, he wanted to send it in writing so that everything will be fixed before his visit, so that when he arrives the time will be enjoyable.

He also encouraged them to have a collection ready for the needy saints in Jerusalem when he comes, so that he can take the collection and send it to Jerusalem.

The reasons why he wrote the letter: to encourage them and show his gratitude to God for their repentance; to defend his apostleship; to rebuke the ungodly behavior that still existed in Corinth, in order not to rebuke them during his visit; and to encourage them to collect money for the needy in Jerusalem.

Most letters by St. Paul have some doctrinal teaching, but this letter is the least doctrinal of St. Paul's letters. In comparison with Romans or Hebrews or some other letters, there is not much doctrine; rather it is about himself and his ministry—a biographical letter. It tells more about St. Paul as a person, as

a servant, and as a minister.

This letter is very good to be studied by servants, because it explains how service should be, as we learn this from the example of St. Paul.

## OUTLINE OF 2 CORINTHIANS

### Chapter 1
• Greeting (1-2)
• Comfort in Suffering (3-7)
• Delivered from Suffering (8-11)
• St. Paul's Sincerity (12-14)
• Sparing the Church (15-24)

### Chapter 2
• Sparing the Church (1-2)
• Forgive the Offender (3-11)
• Triumph in Christ (12-17)

### Chapter 3
• Jesus Christ's Epistle (1-3)
• The Spirit, Not the Letter (4-6)
• Glory of the New Covenant (7-18)

### Chapter 4
• The Light of Christ's Gospel (1-6)
• Cast Down but Unconquered (7-15)
• Seeing the Invisible (16-18)

### Chapter 5
• Assurance of the Resurrection (1-8)
• The Judgment Seat of Christ (9-11)
• Be Reconciled to God (12-21)

# 1

**1:1   Paul, an apostle of Jesus Christ by the will of God.** Paul often described himself as a 'bondservant,' but in this letter he did not label himself as a 'bondservant,' but rather as "an apostle." Why? Because one of the reasons he wrote this letter was to defend his apostleship. He also said, "by the will of God." It is God who called him; God who made him an apostle. St. Paul did not appoint himself to the apostleship, nor was it by the will of men; but it was by the will of God. He is telling them, "If you do not accept my apostleship, it is as if you are not accepting the will of God."

**and Timothy our brother.** Timothy had been sent to Corinth carrying the first letter and had now returned. Because he had spent time with them and delivered a letter to them, St. Timothy also joined St. Paul in greeting them and in writing this letter.

**to the church of God which is at Corinth, with all the saints who are in all Achaia.** This letter was sent to the church of God which is in Corinth, with all the saints who are in all Achaia. "All Achaia" means the whole of Greece – Corinth is part of Greece, so he is sending this letter to all the churches in Greece. Most probably there were some churches existing in Greece, like the Church of Cenchrea and Phoebe, who were neighbors to this church. Not only was there the church in Corinth, but there were also other churches, that is why St. Paul sent this letter mainly to the Church in Corinth, yet all other churches in Greece were also included in this letter

**1:2   Grace to you and peace from God our Father and the Lord Jesus Christ.** St. Paul frequently begins his letters saying, "Grace and peace." If you think about grace and peace, these two gifts are the most needed gifts in everyone's life.   Without the grace of God we cannot achieve anything earthly or heavenly; that is why we need the grace of God. Likewise, in the world we will be exposed to many hardships and tribulations, and we actually need to hold our peace in order to experience this peace in the midst of all these hardships and tribulations. When we pray, let us pray for grace and peace. When we pray for our families, our friends, and our children, let us pray for grace and peace. St. Paul, in almost all of his letters says, "Grace to you, and peace." The world may offer help, it might offer peace, but the Lord told us, "Not as the world gives, do I give you. That is why when he spoke about grace and peace St. Paul clearly stated that he was, "not speaking about the grace and peace of the world, but grace and peace from God our Father and the Lord Jesus Christ." "The Law was given through Moses but grace and truth came through Jesus Christ" (John 1:17). St. Paul was speaking here about the peace and grace that are given to us through our Lord Jesus Christ.

**1:3** **Blessed be the God and Father of our Lord Jesus Christ, the Father of mercies and God of all comfort.** St. Paul started by praising God and blessing Him. Of course as an apostle, it is very suitable to start his letter by blessing God. We bless the Lord and praise Him for so many reasons, but St. Paul is focusing here on one reason. He describes God as "the Father of mercies and God of all comfort." Can you imagine if God took away His mercies from the world for a twinkling of an eye, a fraction of a second – what would happen in this world? It would be a disaster; it would be the end of the world. If God would actually take away His mercies for a fraction of a second, all of us would be destroyed. We live by the mercies of God. I once read a very nice, powerful description of hell. It mentioned that hell is the place where the mercies of God do not exist. As St. James says, there is no mercy to those

who are not merciful (James 2:13) – that is hell. So, if there were no mercies, it would be as if people are enduring the sufferings of hell. Through the mercies of God, we are comforted. Can you imagine if God said, "I will not forgive your sins?" – there is no mercy here – how miserable would we be? But when we sin and come back begging the mercies of God, and God accepts our repentance and gives us His mercies, we feel comforted. That is why in the Divine Liturgy we say, "According to your mercy, O Lord, and not according to our sins." We are essentially saying to God, "If You judge us according to our sins, all of us will be most miserable, that is why we are asking You to judge us not according to our sins, but according to Your mercies, O Lord." Mercies are the fountain of comfort, and comfort is the outward expression of mercy. Because God has mercy on us, we are comforted. That is why St. Paul described God as "the Father of mercies and God of all comfort."

**1:4** **Who comforts us in all our tribulation.** The word "all" is very important. In all our tribulation, not in most of them. If you are going through a difficult time, God will comfort you. If we do not feel comforted, maybe it is because we are closing our door to God. That is why God is standing at the door, knocking, asking us to open the doors of our hearts. Why? To comfort us, to comfort us in all our tribulations. Many times, God does not take us out of the tribulations, but rather comforts us within the tribulation. In the minds of many people, the only way for God to comfort us is to remove the tribulation. However, God may not take away the tribulation, but He will comfort me in the tribulation. God gives comfort in the tribulation and also after the tribulation. So even during the time of affliction and hardship, God is comforting us.

**that we may be able to comfort those who are in any trouble, with the comfort with which we ourselves are comforted by God.** Those who experience the comfort of God during hardship are the most suitable people to comfort others during their hardships. How will they comfort them? St. Paul says, "With the comfort with which we ourselves are comforted by God." In tribulation God comforts us until we are comforted, and not only until we are comforted, but until we have an abundance of this Godly comfort by which we are able to comfort our brethren who suffer. ❋ Allow me to tell you a personal experience here. Believe me, many, many times, when I hear bad news—as in the loss of a loved one, or a very serious disease—as I am on my way to visit the family, I think, "What am I going to say, because there are no words that I can say to comfort these people?" I pray and ask God to be with me during this difficult time, because what do you say to a family

who, for example, has lost their son or their parent? In most of the cases—if not in all of the cases—do you know what happens? When I get there, they comfort me instead of me comforting them. Their words comfort me and at the end I realize what St. Paul said here; that during the time of hardship, God comforts people so that He not only comforts them and gives them consolation, but they are also able to comfort others with this comfort which they received from God. Yes, St. Paul labeled God so truthfully, that He is "the Father of mercies and God of all comfort." Yes indeed, God, our God, is the Father of mercies and God of all comfort.

**1:5 For as the sufferings of Christ abound in us, so our consolation also abounds through Christ.** St. Paul is saying here, "As God allows us to suffer with Him and as the sufferings of Christ abound in us, in the same way the comfort, the consolation of God, will abound in us. I want you to notice here what St. Paul said: "The sufferings of Christ abound in us." Who is 'us' here? It is us during hardship; it is us who suffer. But St. Paul did not say "our suffering." He said, "the sufferings of Christ," because actually, our suffering is His own suffering. Do you remember when the Lord appeared to St. Paul on the road to Damascus (Acts 9)? What did He tell him? "Saul, Saul, why do you persecute Me?" He did not tell him, "Why do you persecute my children the Christians?" He told him, "Why do you persecute Me?" The suffering that My children are enduring, is My own suffering. That is why the comforts of Christ will be our own comfort. If our suffering is His, then His comfort is ours. Christ suffers with us when we suffer for His sake. From what the Lord told him: "Why do you persecute Me?" St. Paul understands that if he endures affliction for Christ, as at Ephesus, then it is as if Christ is the one who endured this suffering, not St. Paul. That is why Christ will comfort those who endure suffering for Him. As Christ actually promised, "They will put you out of the synagogues; yes, the time is coming that whoever kills you will think that he offers God service. And these things they will do to you because they have not known the Father nor Me. But these things I have told you, that when the time comes, you may remember that I told you of them. And these things I did not say to you at the beginning, because I was with you" (John 16:2–4). Then the Lord told them, "I will see you again and you will be joyful, and nobody will take away your joy from you." As the sufferings of Christ abound in us, so our consolation also abounds through Christ! If our sufferings are His, then His consolation will be our consolation, and as the suffering abounds, so also the consolation abounds.

**1:6 Now if we are afflicted, it is for your consolation and salvation.** St. Paul is saying, "When we suffer, it is for your benefit. God will use our suffering for your benefit." How? It will be an example to you when you hear how we endured and how God comforted us and then when you go through hardship, you will endure and be comforted. That is why he said, "If we are afflicted, it is for your consolation and salvation" – "You will see the work of God in our life, and because you will see how God delivered us, you will be comforted and you will be saved."

**which is effective for enduring the same sufferings which we also suffer.** When you are exposed the same suffering, you will also endure. Why will you endure? Because now you have confidence that as God delivered us, He will also deliver you, and so you will willingly accept and endure the suffering.

**Or if we are comforted, it is for your consolation and salvation.** You will know that there is truly a God who takes care of His children, who defends them, who comforts them in their suffering and in their tribulation.

**1:7 And our hope for you is steadfast, because we know that as you are partakers of the sufferings, so also you will partake of the**

**consolation.** St. Paul said that this hope in their being comforted by God in their hardship—this hope is steadfast. He is sure that if they go through difficult times God will comfort them. Why is he so sure? Because this rule will never be broken. Which rule? That if you participate in the sufferings of Christ, you will also participate in the consolation of Christ. That is why he said, "our hope for you"—our hope for what? That you will be delivered in the time of suffering. This hope is steadfast; we are assured of this rule: "That as you are partakers of the sufferings, so also you will partake of the consolation." God is the God of mercies and the Father of compassion, so when you endure the suffering, God will comfort you. ❖ Now St. Paul will give them an example. He will share an experience that happened to him and how God delivered him. Why? He will share the experience of his suffering and the experience of his deliverance in order to encourage, support, and strengthen their faith.

**1:8 For we do not want you to be ignorant, brethren, of our trouble which came to us in Asia.** You can read the details of this trouble in Asia in detail in Acts 19:29–38. It concerns Demetrius and his fellow craftsmen—silversmiths who were concerned for their industry which would go out of business if people no longer worshipped idols. When St. Paul started to preach Christ and people started convert to Christianity, the silversmiths wanted to kill him. If you read Acts 20:1, you will see how St. Paul departed suddenly and secretly from Ephesus, because they wanted to kill him. His sudden departure from Ephesus immediately after the riot shows that he was in real danger. St. Paul explained this danger to us here by saying, "We were burdened beyond measure, above strength, so that we despaired even of life."

**Asia.** He was not speaking of Asia as a continent, but about the Roman province of Asia, which is the western part of Asia Minor. And the capital of these parts was Ephesus.

**that we were burdened beyond measure, above strength, so that we despaired even of life.** These are very serious words coming from the mouth of St. Paul. When St. Paul says beyond measure, above strength, so that we despaired even of life, these are very serious words; it is real danger which St. Paul was exposed to!

**1:9 Yes, we had the sentence of death in ourselves.** He felt that the time had come for him to die. That is why St. Paul said, "Now, as if we had a sentence of death, an order from the king for me to be killed, as if I am awaiting my execution." If a person reaches this level, then he is actually hopeless and helpless. A dead man is hopeless and helpless; he cannot return to life or even cry for help. When a person reaches a level of hopelessness and helplessness, is there a lesson here? Yes. The lesson is: do not depend on yourself, simply because you are hopeless and helpless. But is there hope for the hopeless? Yes, God is the hope of those who have no hope.

**that we should not trust in ourselves but in God who raises the dead.** Here he makes the switch. Instead of trusting yourself, you need to trust who? Trust God, because God is the hope for the hopeless, and He is the help for the helpless. God can raise the dead. Even if they kill me, God can raise me from the dead. I like how St. Paul here, even in the time of despair, was able to not lose hope. Even in the time of hopelessness and helplessness, he was able to not lose hope because he switched the focus to God—God who raises the dead. That is why St. Paul was saying, "My deliverance here, from this trouble, is as a resurrection from death. God delivering me this time, from this tribulation, is as if He has raised me from death." Is God able to do this? Yes.

**1:10**   Who delivered us from

**so great a death, and does deliver us; in whom we trust that He will still deliver us.** St. Paul knew that his death was sure; they were sure to kill him no matter what, but God was able to deliver him from so great a death. He used "delivered" in the past tense, and then "delivers us" in the present tense—"in whom we trust that He will still deliver us," I think this verse is one of the most powerful verses about hope. He delivered us, He does deliver us, in Him we trust that He will still deliver us—past, present, and future. We should not lose hope because God is continuously delivering us from all tribulations. ✷ St. Paul is also teaching us another lesson here: if what will help deliver us is our trust in God, then we should cry out for help and ask God – which is what we know as prayer. That is why we need to pray for one another all the time, but especially during the time of affliction. When St. Peter was in prison, we read in the Book of Acts that the whole church was praying for him..

**1:11 You also helping together in prayer for us.** St. Paul recognized that the prayers of the Corinthian church on his behalf helped him. People prayed for him, and God delivered him through their prayers; this is intercession.

**that thanks may be given by many persons on our behalf for the gift granted to us through many.** When people realized that God delivered St.

Paul, that He accepted their prayers on behalf of St. Paul and delivered him, then their prayer led to thanksgiving. ❈ Prayer leads to joy, joy leads to thanksgiving, and thanksgiving leads to prayer. This way we will end up praying without ceasing, joyful always, and giving thanks in all things. That is what St. Paul is saying here: "When you prayed and God listened to your prayers and delivered me from so great a death, then you became joyful. Because you became joyful, many persons gave thanks on our behalf for the gift of deliverance granted to us through many people." The prayer of many persons secured the gift of his deliverance; hence many could give thanks on behalf of St. Paul.

**1:12   For our boasting is this: the testimony of our conscience.** Beginning with this verse, St. Paul begins to defend his integrity. Here he is saying that his conscience does not blame him. Some people started to cast doubts on St. Paul's integrity, alleging that he was not a man of integrity. They said, "Paul changed his plans to visit you because he is not a man of his word and does not keep his promises. Furthermore, he uses ambiguous words so that you cannot hold him accountable." They were saying that St. Paul used this fleshly, carnal, and earthly wisdom, so that he would not be held accountable. St. Paul responded,

"Actually, if that is what you think of me, let me tell you what my conscience (which is guarded and guided by the Holy Spirit) testifies about us. Here is the testimony of our conscience and I greatly boast in this testimony."

**that we conducted ourselves in the world in simplicity and godly sincerity, not with fleshly wisdom but by the grace of God, and more abundantly toward you.** This is the testimony of St. Paul's conscience. In other words, "I was sincere with you when I told you that I was coming to visit you; I was sincere and my words were simple, plain words. I did not use fleshly wisdom. I did not use ambiguous words or unclear messages. But by the grace of God I was speaking to you, and more abundantly toward you." He boasted that he had acted with purity of purpose, integrity, and under the guidance of God. "If I changed my plan, this was through the guidance of God also; I did not do this on my own, but God guided me," as he would explain in a moment why he changed his plans. He appealed to his singleness of purpose—their salvation—because he was charged with the accusation that he was changing his plan and being ambiguous with his words.

**1:13   For we are not writing any other things to you than what you read or understand. Now I trust you will understand, even to the**

**end.** He told them, "What you have read and what you have understood is what we wrote to you. We used plain words, words that do not have double meaning." Sometimes people use words that have two meanings and each person takes the meaning that they want, but St. Paul said, "No, I do not do this. Now I trust that you will understand, even to the end." He insisted on writing plainly so that they may understand and accept what he wrote. He was appealing to them to understand what he wrote to them, to the end. Do not try to dig deep behind his words; "What I write to you is what I meant. There are no hidden messages; I do not send to you a hidden message. And I trust that you will understand this even to the end, in listening to me, try to understand that I am writing to you plainly and clearly."

**1:14 (As also you have understood us in part).** "Some of you have understood that we are simple, that we are sincere, that we are men of integrity; not all of you. Some of you—actually the majority of you—acknowledged us as men of integrity, as apostles, and rejoiced in our service and labor."

**that we are your boast as you also are ours, in the day of the Lord Jesus.** You boast in us and we boast in you, when Christ comes. This would be a wonderful relationship between the pastor or priest and his congregation. In the day of the coming of the Lord Jesus Christ, the clergy and the servants should boast in their people, because as St. Paul said, you are our crown, our joy. When a person invents something, he boasts in the invention and the design that he made. Many architects, after designing a beautiful church or building, boast in this building. In the same way, you are our service, our work, so at the coming of our Lord Jesus Christ, we hope to, as we should, boast in you. In the same way, you should boast in us; you should be proud that, "St. Paul is our teacher, St. Paul is our founder." The boasting here in the day of our Lord Jesus Christ should be mutual—the pastor boasting in his people and the people boasting in their shepherd.

**1:15 And in this confidence I intended to come to you before, that you might have a second benefit.** Which confidence? That they acknowledged his apostleship and rejoiced in his labor. "You benefited from my first visit and now you have a second benefit," as it was the second visit. So, "Because of this confidence— that you boast in us and I boast in you— by which you acknowledge me as an apostle and you acknowledge me as sent by the Lord Jesus Christ and you rejoice in my labor—in this confidence I intended to come to you, and this intention was real. My plan when I told you I was coming to visit you was a truthful plan."

**1:16** **To pass by way of you to Macedonia, to come again from Macedonia to you, and be helped by you on my way to Judea.** He went directly to Macedonia, although he had planned to stop at Corinth first then go to Macedonia. His plan was to stop by them on his way to Macedonia, and then on his way back from Macedonia to Judea (sailing straight across from Ephesus to Corinth) he would stop back at Corinth again.

**1:17** **Therefore, when I was planning this, did I do it lightly.** Here St. Paul began to defend himself saying, "Did I plan lightly? Was I not serious in my planning? I did not take it lightly, as you presume."

**Or the things I plan, do I plan according to the flesh, that with me there should be Yes, Yes, and No, No?** What did St. Paul mean by, "Or the things I plan, do I plan according to the flesh?" Am I using earthly wisdom? Will I tell you that I am coming to visit you while I am not actually coming? "Do I plan according to the flesh, that with me there should be Yes, Yes, and No, No?" Meaning my "yes" could be "no" and my "no" could be "yes?" This is fleshly wisdom. Apparently, the

people in Corinth heard of his plans. We understand from 1 Corinthians 5 that there was a letter sent from St. Paul to Corinth, but this letter was not added. Perhaps he told them about his plans in this letter, then he actually declared to them that he had changed his plan. So, people started to accuse him of this indecisiveness, that he took things lightly – that he was not taking people seriously enough, and that his "yes" could be "no" and his "no" could be "yes.".

**1:18** **But as God is faithful, our word to you was not Yes and No.** He said, "No, we are not men who would give you confusing messages. As God is faithful to us, so our message to you is also 'yes' or 'no.' When we say 'yes,' we intend yes, when we say 'no,' we intend no; it is never yes and no at the same time." Their word was not ambiguous or unreliable.

The idea here is that there was no indecisiveness or uncertainty on his part; how would St. Paul be trusted by God to preach the word of the Gospel if he used carnal wisdom? If his "yes" was "no" and his "no" was "yes," then how could God trust St. Paul to preach the Gospel?.

**1:19** **For the Son of God, Jesus Christ, who was preached among you by us—by me, Silvanus, and Timothy—was not Yes and No, but in Him was Yes.** "Us" includes Paul, Silvanus, and Timothy. "When we preached Christ or told you that Christ is God, this was not yes and no; it would be a disaster if this was yes and no – that would mean 'Christ is God' and 'Christ is not God.'" In essence, St. Paul was telling them, "If my 'Yes' could be 'No,' then my preaching also could be 'No!' So, if we preached 'Christ is God,' that maybe He is not God, this is not the case! 'Yes, Christ is God,' and I have two witnesses with me – Silvanus and Timothy."

**but in Him was Yes.** In other words, "All the promises that we told you, all the teaching, all the preaching, are true."

**1:20** **For all the promises of God in Him are Yes, and in Him Amen, to the glory of God through us.** "If we told you that God will deliver you, then this is 'Yes and amen'; it will never be 'No.' All the promises, all the preaching are, 'Yes and amen,' otherwise, how

will God be glorified? If I tell you that God will deliver you but He does not? God will be glorified for the glory of God through us, through our ministry." All the promises of God are sure and positive. "If God entrusted us to preach the message of the Gospel, which is the Truth with a capital 'T,' then we are men of integrity and we will not use 'Yes' and 'No' language to confuse you or to send hidden messages."

**1:21** **Now He who establishes us with you in Christ and has anointed us is God.** Who gave us integrity? Who made us men of promise? It is God. He who established us with you in Christ, confirmed us with you in Christ, and anointed us by the Holy Spirit, is God. As God established us, made us steadfast in Christ, confirmed us in Him, and as Christ, as God has established you also, so He has established us too. It is God who gave us our stability, so that our work is yes, sure, and steadfast. St. Paul was comparing here between faith and his words. The establishment that he was talking about here is being established in faith—when you accepted Christ, who made you stable in your faith, were you not shaken even by persecution? It is God; God has not established us only, but has also established you. How did He establish us? Through the anointing of the Holy Spirit, through the grace of the Holy Spirit.

**1:22** **Who also has sealed us and given us the Spirit in our hearts as a guarantee.** When you seal something that means it belongs to you, you own it. God sealed us by the Holy Spirit – that is established. Then the promise of the inheritance of the Kingdom of God is sure and steadfast. You know how you put earnest in money? Similarly, we are sealed and not only this, but God gave us the guarantee. What is the guarantee? His Spirit—He gave us the Holy Spirit to dwell in us when we were anointed with the holy oil. The idea here is: "How do you doubt our words? If you doubt our words, then you are actually doubting our faith, and if you are doubting our faith and preaching, then you are doubting the Holy Spirit, because God – the Holy Spirit – is the One who established us. So how do you doubt my words yet you say that my "Yes" is "No" and my "No" is "Yes?" They cannot doubt his faith and that of his fellows, Silvanus and Timothy, without doing injury to the Spirit of God. "As God established us in faith, as God sealed us and gave us the Holy Spirit as a guarantee, He also gave us this promise that we are His children, His own people, and gave us the inheritance of the Kingdom of God, and this seal is guaranteed by the gift of the Holy Spirit in our hearts." The words of St. Paul were yes; he was not using unclear or ambiguous messages.

**1:23** **Moreover I call God as witness against my soul.** Now he explained to them why he changed his plan. Lest they think that he was making an excuse he said, "I call on God to witness against me. God knows the truth about why I changed my plan. Not because I am not a man of word or promise, not due to indecisiveness or because I took you lightly, but to spare you.

**that to spare you I came no more to Corinth.** He wanted to spare them by giving them time after reading the first Letter to repent, so that when he went to visit them he would not rebuke them, and it would be a joyful visit. That is why he told them, "to spare you I came no more to Corinth, to give you time to repent and to fix the things that are going wrong in the church." But here, "to spare you," implies what? That he might discipline them if they continue to do wrong.

**1:24** **Not that we have dominion over your faith.** After his remarks in the previous verse, St. Paul provides clarity in case people perceive him as expressing dominion or making himself a lord over them.

**but are fellow workers for your joy.** What does he mean by "for your joy?" "If I discipline you in order to lead you to repentance, then with repentance comes the joy of salvation. When I discipline you, it is not because of dominion or because of lordship; I understand my ministry – I am a fellow worker, I am a helper, I am a servant for your joy. Therefore, when I bestow such pain, when I bestow in you such discipline, I am helping your faith, I am advancing your faith, I am promoting your faith, which is the source of all joy," as we read in Romans 15:31.

**for by faith you stand.** "Why do I want to help your faith? Why do I want to advance your faith? Why do I want to promote your faith? Because by faith you stand, by faith you will have joy. That is why I am helping you with your faith. I want nothing from you. I do not want to lord it over you or to have dominion over you, but I want to help you to be joyful. So, when I changed my plan, my intention was to spare you – spare you this discipline, to give you time to repent and fix things, so that when I come to you and visit you it will be an enjoyable visit and a pleasurable visit."

## Chapter 1 Questions

1. Does God provide comfort in only one state of tribulation or all?

2. What role did the believers play while the apostle was suffering in Asia?

3. Where did St. Paul suffer?

4. In the day of the Lord, what will be the relationship between the servants and the believers?

5. What kind of help did St. Paul require of the believers?

6. How does St. Paul make plans?

7. Who established St. Paul and anointed the believers?

# 2

## Chapter Outline

**2:1  But I determined this within myself, that I would not come again to you in sorrow.** The word "again" here is very important. The desire of St. Paul was not to rebuke them, but to go and rejoice with them. That is why he changed his plan and waited until they had repented and changed their attitude. He did this so that when he visited them, he would rejoice with them; not to rebuke them or make them sorrowful, but to rejoice with them. Actually, the word "again" means that there was a time when he visited them in heaviness of heart, and that visit was not recorded for us in the Book of Acts. The word "again" in this verse implies that St. Paul probably visited them while he was preaching at Ephesus — across the sea – perhaps for two or three days. There are some other verses that support this visit, like 2 Corinthians 12:14 and 21, and also 2 Corinthians 13:1. From these verses we can conclude that St. Paul visited them and rebuked them. This visit was like a heavy visit, a visit of sorrow and grief because he had rebuked them. That is why he changed

his plan; he did not want to go to them again in heaviness, but rather after they had repented so that they would have a joyful time together.

**2:2  For if I make you sorrowful, then who is he who makes me glad but the one who is made sorrowful by me.** St. Paul was responding to speculation here. Perhaps some people had said, "No, this is not enough reason to change your plan, since you actually showed no regret in causing heaviness and causing sorrow during your visit while you were in Ephesus." Perhaps some people had questioned St. Paul and his integrity saying, "But the last visit you made to us, you actually did make us sorrowful, rebuked us, and made us heavy, so this is not the real reason that you want to come to us and rejoice with us." St. Paul answers in this verse saying: "If I am the one to cause you sorrow, it is not that I have any pleasure in doing so. If I made you sorrowful, rest assured that I have no pleasure in making you sorrowful or causing you to grieve, but my objective was that he who was made sorry by me, should repent, and so make me and all of you glad. So, to make you sorrowful is not my goal, to make you grieve is not my goal, but if this is the tool that I need to use in order for you to repent, I will use it because I care about your repentance. Then when you actually repent, you will make me glad, and also make every one else glad. So, your sorrow, in a way, gladdens me, on account of your repentance. Your sorrow made me glad, because through this sorrow you repented." That is what he meant: "My intention is not to make you sorrowful, but my intention is to lead you to repentance, thus you will make me happy and make everybody else happy by your repentance."

**2:3** **And I wrote this very thing to you, lest, when I came, I should have sorrow over those from whom I ought to have joy, having confidence in you all that my joy is the joy of you all.** "This very thing" refers to the postponement of his visit to Corinth. He is telling them, "I wrote to you about my change of plans (in 1 Corinthians 16:5) having confidence that you will repent. If I did not have confidence that you would repent, there would have been no reason for me to change my plans. I would have needed to come to encourage you to repent; I have confidence that you will repent, so that we may all rejoice together." "So, why did I make this plan? Because I have confidence in you all, that my joy is the joy of you all." He trusted that they too would feel that there was sufficient reason for the postponement, if this would interfere with their mutual joy. He was telling them, "I have confidence that you will repent, I have confidence that you will understand why I changed my plan. Because we need to have joyful memories together, I have given

you this time to repent so that when I visit you, my visit to you will be a time in which all of us will rejoice together."

**2:4** **For out of much affliction and anguish of heart I wrote to you, with many tears, not that you should be grieved, but that you might know the love which I have so abundantly for you.** By saying, "I wrote," St. Paul was referring to the first Epistle in which he rebuked them for their problems, divisions, and sexual immorality. He was explaining, "I want you to know that when I wrote this letter to rebuke you, I wrote it with tears, with anguish of heart – I wrote it with affliction. I was not happy to write such a letter to you. Yes, I wrote sharply, but in great sorrow, and not to grieve you, but my goal was to demonstrate my love towards you, my love which was growing abundantly toward you. Because I loved you to that degree, this was why I rebuked you, because I couldn't see you living in such sin without leading you to repentance, and leading you to return to God. This letter, the harsh rebuke, shows you my attentive care for you."

**2:5** **But if anyone has caused grief, he has not grieved me.** "But if anyone has caused grief." Although all the Corinthians have divisions and splits and conflicts, in this verse St.

Paul was referring to the person whom he excommunicated, the person who committed sexual immorality. He said about this person: "he has not grieved me but all of you. He did not only grieve me alone, but he also grieved the whole church."

**but all of you to some extent.** He has repented, so the grief was temporary; if this person, God forbid, had not repented, then the grief would have been be full. He told them that this grief was only to some extent, because he repented.

**not to be too severe.** St. Paul said, "Now I do not want to speak much about his sin"—he actually did not even mention that he had committed sexual immorality; he was covering over his sin as if saying, "I do not want to be too severe on him." Why? Because he has repented. So now there is no reason to be severe on him. "Yes, in my first epistle in Chapter 5, I was harsh on him, I excommunicated him, I delivered him to Satan, but now there is no reason to be too severe on him; he repented." That is why he said, "to some extent—not to be too severe."

Currently, excommunication means that the person does not take communion, but the proper excommunication, which was practiced in the early church, meant no communication; no communication at all. The church cannot greet this person, talk with this person, it was like being in total isolation, and this is what led this person to repentance.

**which was inflicted by the majority.** If the people were communicating with him, then the excommunication would be ineffective. They cut all sorts of communication with this person, and this in itself led the person to repent. This was why St. Paul told them, "You, the whole church, took the action." Under the direction of St. Paul, it was endorsed by the whole church.

**is sufficient for such a man.** St. Paul is now saying, "This punishment is enough for him," because, what is the purpose of punishment? What is the purpose of discipline? It is to lead the person to repentance, and this person has repented. So now, there is no reason for the punishment. Punishment is like medication; if the medication heals the person, then there is no reason to continue giving the medication.

**2:6     This punishment.** "This punishment" is referring to the excommunication which we read about in 1 Corinthians 5:4–5. He added, "This excommunication was not only by me, but by the whole church."

**2:7     so that, on the contrary, you ought rather to forgive and comfort him, lest perhaps such a one be swallowed up with too much sorrow.** "So that, on the contrary" – I want you to do the exact opposite; before you had no communication with him, but now, on the contrary, "you ought rather to forgive and comfort him." "Not only to forgive him, not only to accept him, but to show him much love and to comfort him, because I am concerned lest perhaps such a one be swallowed up with too much grief and sorrow." The goal of punishment is not to destroy the person; it is to bring the person to Christ and to repentance. As St. Paul firmly commanded excommunication of this person, or now he tenderly, encourages them to forgive and comfort him. When St. Paul punished him—you can read this in 1 Corinthians 5:5—he explained clearly that the goal of punishment is to save him. ✤ I urge parents, when they discipline their children, to keep this in mind: discipline to save, not to destroy. I urge the fathers, the priests, I urge everyone who is in charge, if you punish and discipline, keep in mind that we punish not to destroy, but to save and lead the person to repentance.

**2:8 Therefore I urge you to reaffirm your love to him.** In other words: "After having had no communication with him, now I want you to communicate with him, and not only to communicate with him, but to communicate lovingly with him, to reaffirm your love to him so that he will know that this punishment was not out of hatred, but out of love. This discipline was not because we hated, judged, or condemned him, but out of love in order to bring him to repentance."

**2:9 For to this end I also wrote, that I might put you to the test, whether you are obedient in all things.** St. Paul gave them another reason why they should restore this person. The first reason was lest this person is swallowed up in sorrow and the second reason was, "I want this to be a proof of your obedience to the church." ✤ Why did St. Paul want them to obey him? Was it something related to his ego and pride? Certainly not! Obeying our father the priest, obeying the clergy, is actually a sign of our obedience to God. As the Lord said, "Those who obey you, obey me" (John 15:20). Because the rule in the church is not democratic nor is it dictatorship; the rule in the church is, Theocratic. "Theo" is Greek for "God"; God is ruling through the clergy. God is ruling through His ministers and His servants, thus our obedience to our clergy is actually our obedience to God. ✤ St. Paul wanted to test their obedience. He asked them to excommunicate him and they followed through with it. Perhaps they had excommunicated him because he had brought shame (seeking revenge in their hearts), so when St. Paul told them to excommunicate him, they responded, wanting vengeance on this person who had brought shame to the church in Corinth. But when St. Paul tested their obedience, asking them to reaffirm their love to him, if the excommunication had been out of vengeance, they would have not obeyed St. Paul, but because they obeyed him, everybody reaffirmed their love to this offender. This is why he said, "Whether you are obedient in all things"—previously, in punishing him, in excommunicating him, and now, in loving him.

**2:10   Now whom you forgive anything, I also forgive. For if indeed I have forgiven anything, I have forgiven that one for your sakes in the presence of Christ.** Now he told them, "As your excommunication of the offender was my act, so also your restoration of him will be my act; if you forgive him, I will forgive him. First, I excommunicated him and you supported me, now forgive him and I will support you." That is why he said, "It is for your sakes that I have forgiven, and I do forgive."And the third reason why he forgave him is so the church may suffer no hurt by the loss of this soul. How? St. Paul explained this: "Now whom you forgive anything, I also forgive." Meaning, "we work in harmony—if you forgive, I will forgive, if I excommunicate, you will excommunicate; whom you forgive anything, I also forgive."

**for your sakes.** St. Paul elaborates further in verse 11 regarding what he means when he says "for your sakes":

**2:11   Lest Satan should take advantage of us; for we are not ignorant of his devices.** This was the third reason why he forgave that person: lest Satan should take advantage of us. If the church had continued the excommunication of this person, the church would have suffered the loss of one person – one person from the hundred sheep would be lost. Recall that the Lord told us to leave the 99 and search for the lost sheep. St. Paul was instructing them so that "the church may suffer no hurt by the loss of this one soul. Just as you learned a lesson in faithfulness, I want you to learn a lesson in compassion. As you were being faithful to Christ and excommunicated the person who offended the church, now I want you to learn a lesson in compassion—how to be compassionate to this person." "I am exercising this excommunication and restoration as an apostle of Christ, who has the authority of Christ." This is why he said, "In the presence of Christ (in the previous verse)—I am representing Christ and acting by the authority of Christ, because we are the stewards of God." "If you allow this person to be lost through despair, then we are actually giving Satan a weapon to attack the church." If we, by our repulsive harshness, do not accept the repentant person, we are actually handing this person over to Satan. Remember in 1 Corinthians 5:5, St. Paul delivered this person to Satan saying, "I delivered such a one to Satan for the destruction of the flesh, that his spirit may be saved." What did he mean by "the destruction of the flesh?" Destruction of the flesh occurs when nobody communicates with this person and so this person suffers grief. All this grief and suffering attacks his flesh, while his spirit yearns for repentance and returning to God and to communion with the church. Perhaps he is asking that the grace of God be taken away from his flesh, that he may experience suffering here on earth—maybe his flesh will suffer from diseases or from some hardships or tribulations—and that through all these tribulations, including the excommunication, he would return to God and repent so that his spirit will be saved. If they had not accepted him, then they not only would have delivered his flesh to Satan, but they also would have delivered his soul and his spirit to Satan, which is what Satan wants. The desire of Satan is to destroy the spirit also, and if we do not accept the repentant person, it is as if we are giving Satan an advantage over each of us. St. Paul said, "For we are not ignorant of his devices." We know very well the plans and tricks of Satan. We know how Satan wants to destroy the spirit; one of the means he uses is despair. That is actually how Satan destroyed the spirit of Judas Iscariot—he made him lose hope and fall into despair. When we refuse to accept and restore the repentant sinner, we are actually making this person fall in despair, and thus, we are giving an opportunity to Satan to destroy the spirit of this person by hopelessness. St. Paul said, "I am asking you to accept him

and show him love for three reasons: (1) lest this person be swallowed up in sorrow, (2) to test your obedience, and (3) lest we give an opportunity to Satan to destroy the soul of this person." What is the goal of the church? "The Son of man did not come to condemn the world, but to save the world," (cf 9:56) and we should be working with God to save people, not to destroy them.

**2:12** Beginning with this this verse, St. Paul changed his tone. The tone had been about sorrow, punishment, grief, excommunication, but as St. Paul said in Romans 8, "All things work together for the glory of God" (Romans 8:28). So, even this excommunication, even this sorrow, turned to be an opportunity for joy. Satan was defeated, and Christ, through gaining the soul of this person, is victorious. Now the image that St. Paul gives is Christ leading us in a victorious procession of triumph, because we have won the soul of this offender, not giving opportunity to Satan to win this soul; Christ won this soul. That is why St. Paul gave thanks to God, who leads us at all times and through all ways in the procession of victory and triumph.

**Furthermore, when I came to Troas to preach Christ's gospel.** St. Paul expected to meet Titus at Troas. After he had sent the letter of first Corinthians in which he rebuked them harshly, St. Paul was worried how they would receive and react to this letter, so he then sent Titus and told him, "Meet me at Troas. Bring me news. I want to know how the church in Corinth is doing." He expected to meet Titus in Troas to receive the news of how they responded to the first Letter to the Corinthians, but he was disappointed in his expectation because Titus did not come to Troas; St. Paul passed on to Macedonia, where he met them at last. But he "had no rest in his spirit," and actually, this shows us the tender heart of St. Paul. He rebuked but he, in his heart, had no rest, because these are his children! The person whom he excommunicated is his son! His plan was not to destroy him; he wanted him to return back to Christ. ❧ Often as Sunday school servants, priest, or parents, we rebuke harshly, and maybe our intention is to bring somebody to Christ, but afterwards, we should not completely sever communication with this person, we should ask about him, as this is the attitude of a real pastor; this is the attitude of a real servant of Christ. If you rebuke someone harshly for his repentance, you should not have rest in your heart, like St. Paul, until you hear good news of the situation and salvation of this person. Although the Lord opened a door for ministry to St. Paul, he did not have rest in his heart until he knew the good news from Titus. Actually, the Book of Acts does not record for us that he passed through Troas when going from Ephesus to Macedonia, but it does record for us how St. Paul started in Troas when he returned from Macedonia. It is apparent

from this verse that St. Paul did stop in Troas but he did not meet Titus there, which may be why he moved quickly. In Acts 20:7 we read that he had disciples in Troas. During his visit to Troas, he made some disciples, so when he returned from Macedonia and stopped in Troas, he met with those disciples. The Lord had opened a door for St. Paul there, and he converted some people to Christianity.

**and a door was opened to me by the Lord.** St. Paul is referring to a figurative "door" in this work. This door was opened by the gracious providence of the Lord; it is not by my effort, it is not because I am an eloquent speaker that the door was opened, but this door was opened by the gracious providence of God. Here some people might ask a very important question: the Lord opened a door for ministry, so would it not have been better for St. Paul to stay at Troas and serve? Should he leave this door which the Lord has opened to him for one single person, in order to hear news about one single person? To answer this question, I would like to remind you of Acts 8, where we read about how Philip did wonderful ministry in Samaria. There was great joy in the city, many people converted to Christianity, and even Simon the sorcerer believed and was baptized. We read in Acts 8: "There was great joy in that city," but then what happened? The Holy Spirit took Philip from this successful ministry and sent him to Gaza, which was a deserted place. Why? For one person—

the Ethiopian eunuch. God cares about the single soul as much as He cares about all of us. For that one person, the Ethiopian eunuch, God asked Philip to leave the 99, the successful ministry in Samaria, and go to this one person. In the same way, St. Paul here left the 99, the door which was open in Troas, for one single person. ❖ Here I have a word to say to the fathers, the priests. As you know, we have communities and we have established churches. These communities might have only one family, three families, four families, and many times we, the priests, say, "Should I leave this church on Friday and Saturday, just to go for one family or a few families? Maybe if I stay here it would be more fruitful." This is why there are many cancellations for community services. But if you think about it, God commanded us to leave the 99 and search for the one soul. Actually, here (in these larger communities) the liturgy is established and they have service every week, having service sometimes even during the weekdays, but these communities have one single service, perhaps once a month. If you cancel this one service, that means the community will stay for two months without a single service! So, if you are tempted to think, "No, I will stay with this bigger church. No, I will bear more fruit here," remember Acts 8, remember what St. Paul did. He left Troas with the opened door there, just for one soul. In the same way, we should be motivated to keep our schedule of community service in order to serve these few

families who have no church close by them. That is why, though a wide door of Christian usefulness opened in Troas for St. Paul, his eagerness to hear the news of Corinth from Titus led him to hasten to Macedonia to meet Titus there.

**2:13** **I had no rest in my spirit, because I did not find Titus my brother; but taking my leave of them, I departed for Macedonia.** Note the spirit of St. Paul was led by the Holy Spirit. So this decision to leave Troas and go to Macedonia to meet Titus was a decision made by the Holy Spirit, because our spirits are led by the Holy Spirit. That is why under the direction of the Holy Spirit, St. Paul was convinced that it was not necessary to stay in Troas, but to go to Macedonia in order to be assured about this person who had been excommunicated. It may be that St. Paul had needed to go back to Corinth to speak to this person or bring him to repentance. Note his humbleness, in that although Titus was his disciple, St. Paul addressed him as his brother.

**2:14** **Now thanks be to God.** that Satan had not won this person, but Christ who had victory over him. "Now thanks be to God that I had met Titus there and heard the good news about the repentance of this person, about how the unity was restored in the church of Corinth, how there are no conflicts nor divisions or schisms there, but everyone is back in union. Now we give thanks to God who always gives us the final victory through Christ." .

**who always leads us in triumph in Christ.** Do not be defeated, do not lose hope, because Christ always leads us in triumph! If you abide in Christ and Christ abides in you, regardless of the challenges or obstacles set before you, regardless of the hindrances before you, you will end in victory and in triumph God always leads us in triumph in Christ.

**and through us diffuses the fragrance of His knowledge in every place.** St. Paul is grateful to God who always gives us victory through Christ, and through us diffuses the fragrance of knowledge in every place. The knowledge of Christ has a fragrance, the knowledge of Christ has a sweet aroma, the knowledge of Christ has a good smell, and through us, this aroma is diffused. Through us, the aroma of the knowledge of Christ is spread among people. ✤ St. Paul had in mind the triumphal procession of the victorious generals. The approach of the procession was recognized by the odor of incense. They would scatter incense so that when the people smelt the incense, they would know that the procession was approaching. St. Paul was saying, "God makes manifest by us the sweet savor of the knowledge of Christ, who is our

triumphant conqueror, everywhere." What did St. Paul mean by this? St. Paul was saying that when people know us, we emit the sweet aroma of Christ. When people see our repentance, unity, love for one another, communion, our fellowship, and when they smell the sweet aroma of the knowledge of Christ in us, they will believe in Christ—the triumphant Conqueror who is leading this procession. St. Paul was saying that we, the Christians, are the incense, the sweet aroma, and when people smell it, they know that Christ is close to them—the procession of Christ, this victorious procession is approaching their hearts, is coming to knock on their hearts, and so they will open their hearts and receive Him as their Lord and Savior. This procession will not only strike their eyes but will also strike their nostrils; every sense feels the power of the Christ-gospel. When people actually smell the love, the unity, the service, the fellowship, the community, the humbleness, they will believe in Christ.

**2:15** **For we are to God the fragrance of Christ among those who are being saved and among those who are perishing.** Here, St. Paul is saying that we not only scatter the fragrance, but we ourselves are the fragrance of Christ. We not only diffuse the sweet aroma of Christ, but we ourselves are the sweet aroma itself.

How are we the fragrance of Christ? Among those who are saved, that is easy to understand, but how are we the fragrance of Christ among those who are perishing? St. John Chrysostom said, "And the light, though it blinds in darkness the weak, is for all still light." Light can actually hurt people who have weak eyes, and can actually blind them in darkness, though it is still light. St. John Chrysostom said, "And as honey, though it tastes bitter to the sick, is in itself still sweet." In the same way, the Gospel still has a sweet savor, though many will perish through not believing the Gospel of Christ. This Gospel is a sweet aroma in itself, but for those who reject Christ and do not accept Him, unfortunately and sadly, this sweet aroma will be an odor to death—not to life. In the Greek procession of victory, the conquered enemies were led in a procession and when the procession ended at the capital, the enemies were killed. So, these conquered people—the defeated people here—were also in the procession, and when they smelled the incense, they knew that their death was near. St. Paul used the same image while saying, "This procession has people who are saved, but also has people who are perishing if they rejected Christ. As the incense to the victorious was an aroma of life, so the same incense was a sign to the enemies that their slaughter was at hand. To them, the smell of incense was the aroma of death leading to death, while to those saved, it was an aroma of life. The Gospel was in the same manner to the different classes, respectively.

**2:16 To the one we are the aroma of death leading to death, and to the other the aroma of life leading to life.** To those who smell the sweet aroma of Christ in us but reject Christ, we are an aroma to death, because they will be condemned at the last day. God will tell them, "I sent you My message, I sent you My children to witness to you but you rejected Me. Depart from Me you evildoers, I do not know you." This odor will be an aroma of death leading to death, but unto the others, an aroma of life leading to life. How do unbelievers perceive the knowledge of Christ? As a mere announcement of a dead Christ and a lifeless Gospel. For them Christ is dead. He was a prophet who died, making the knowledge of Christ a law of death, and the Gospel— the word of God—a lifeless Gospel. That is why it is an aroma of death ending in death, but for those who are saved it is an announcement of a living Christ, the living Savior; thus it is an eternal life.

**And who is sufficient for these things.** As St. Paul reflected on this procession he said, "And who is sufficient for these things? Who is sufficient for diffusing aright everywhere the savor of Christ? What a responsibility on our shoulders to diffuse to others the sweet aroma of the knowledge of Christ! Who is sufficient for this task? Who is sufficiently able to tell people how sweet and how beautiful the knowledge of Christ is?" St. Paul is wondering who is sufficient for these things, this aroma, which is so diverse in its effect on believers and unbelievers.Now St. Paul prepared the way to defend his apostolic mission and his apostolic authority from its attackers in Corinth, who denied his sufficiency. Many people actually said that St. Paul was not sufficient for this ministry and that St. Paul, because he did not see Christ, (he was not one of the Twelve) could not be counted among the apostles. St. Paul said, "You know what? I agree with you. Who is sufficient for this ministry? I am not sufficient to diffuse the fragrance of Christ, the fragrance of the knowledge of Christ to people." In Chapter 3 he answers this question beautifully: "Not that we are sufficient of ourselves…" I agree with you, I am not sufficient for this task, "… but our sufficiency is from God, who also made us sufficient as ministers…" So, if I am speaking, am I sufficient? I am not, but our sufficiency is from God. It is God who also made us sufficient as apostles, as clergy, as ministers, as His pastors

**2:17   For we are not, as so many.** "We—the ministers of Christ, the apostles of Christ— are not as so many…," as the false teachers.

**peddling the word of God; but**

**as of sincerity, but as from God.** "Peddling" means to adulterate. When we were with Pope Shenouda, he explained to us the word "adultery." He told us that adultery comes from two words: 'ad,' which means adding, 'alter' means another, so adultery is like 'adding another.' In marriage when somebody cheats, he is adding another person in this oneness – 'the two shall become one' – that is why it is called adultery. But the verse about weights (unjust weights) also means to add another, likewise to mix wine with water, because we are adding another substance. In Greece, many people adulterated wine for gain, so he is referring to the Judaizers, the false teachers who wanted to add the Jewish tradition to the pure Gospel, and so to add to the Gospel of Christ the indictments of Judaism. He said, "We are not like them, we are not like so many false teachers deadening the word of God. Not so, but on the contrary, me and my fellow teachers speak the word with sincerity and with a sense of responsibility toward God." That is why he said, "We are not … peddling the word of God; but as of sincerity, but as from God, we speak in the sight of God in Christ." And so these words, we do not change them. What we deliver to you was received from God.

**we speak in the sight of God in Christ.** We know that God is observing us. We know that God is watching every word we say, and we are saying these words in Christ. These words that we received in Christ are given to us by Christ and are approved by Christ, so we are not like so many false teachers." Here St. Paul was defending his ministry because as I told you, many people attacked him and said that he was not sufficient to be an apostle. And so St. Paul said, "Yes, I agree, who is sufficient for these things? But our sufficiency is not from us; it is from God, and that is why the word we are giving is the word of Christ. We give it to you with all sincerity and in the sight of God. Know that we are accountable before God,"

## Chapter 2 Questions

1. In this chapter, St Paul forgave a man who had sinned. Where in the bible was the story of this man mentioned?

2. What would have been the danger awaiting that man if he was left for a longer time without forgiveness?

3. In verse 9, St Paul says "obedient in all things." This refers to two acts by the people of Corinth, one that had already happened, and another yet to happen. What are these two acts?

4. Although St Paul had the apostolic authority, he put himself as equal to the people of Corinth. What is the reference of that in the chapter?

5. In presenting the man's case to the people of Corinth, how did he make sure that they will forgive him?

6. "Because we are not ignorant of his devices." What does this verse mean in the light of the sinner's story?

7. God comforts His followers during their hardships by different means, sometimes through other people. How is this shown in the chapter?

8. What would be the result of enduring hardships joyfully? The word of God is effective and powerful, regardless of people's reaction to it. What verse in this chapter confirms this truth?

9. God's servants that are entrusted with His word may at times corrupt the word. How can they do that?

# 3

## Chapter Outline

**3:1 Do we begin again to commend ourselves? Or do we need, as some others, epistles of commendation to you or letters of commendation from you.** St. Paul wanted to tell them, "Do I need to boast, praise myself, praise my service among you, in order for you to believe that, yes, I am an apostle of the Lord Jesus Christ? Do I need to have a letter of recommendation from the church in Jerusalem?" This was actually a custom, to send a letter of recommendation from the church of Jerusalem, as was done after the first church of Jerusalem in Acts 15, when they sent Paul and Barnabas with the resolution of the Council; they were sent with a letter of commendation. St. Paul is telling them, "After I preached Christ to you, established the church in Corinth, and many of you believed in Christ, do I until now need a letter of recommendation to you or from you?"

**3:2 You are our epistle ... known and read by all men.** The church in Corinth owed its existence to St. Paul. It was as if St. Paul was saying, "The fact that there is a church in Corinth, which I have established and founded, testifies that I am an apostle to the Lord Jesus Christ." His work, his ministry in Corinth was the letter of recommendation.

**written in our hearts.** when he actually looked into his heart, he saw all his children in Corinth written in his heart. And now he is wondering, "You are written in my heart, you are my fruit in Jesus Christ, but you still want a letter of recommendation to tell you that I am an apostle to the Lord Jesus Christ!"

**3:3 Clearly you are an epistle of Christ, ministered by us.** Who wrote the epistle? Who is the real founder of the Church? The church is built on the foundation of Christ; Christ is the Cornerstone. But what is the role of St. Paul? St. Paul was like the pen in the hand of God, but God, the Lord Jesus Christ, is the Author.

**written not with ink but by the Spirit of the living God, not on tablets of stone but on tablets of flesh, that is, of the heart.** Here he was comparing between the Old and New Covenant. The Old Covenant was written by engraving on two tablets of stone, but with the Spirit of God, the tablets here are the hearts of the people. The Holy Spirit used St. Paul to write the Law of God, to write the Covenant on the hearts of the people. In the Old Testament, the Commandments were written on tablets of stone, which indicated that the hearts of the people were like stones and were hardened. In Ezekiel, speaking of the New Covenant, God told us, "I will take the heart of stone out of your flesh and give you a heart of flesh" (Ezekiel 36:26). The Old Covenant was written on hearts of stone, but the New Covenant because of the grace and Spirit of God, is written on hearts of flesh. If there is a stone and I shoot an arrow toward this stone, what will happen? The arrow will break. But if there is a piece of flesh and I shoot an arrow toward this piece of flesh, it will pierce the flesh. In the Old Testament the peoples' hearts were like stone, and the word of God was like an arrow. The arrow hit the hearts of the people and it was broken; that is why they broke the Commandment of God. But in the New Testament as is written in Acts 2, "When they heard, they were pierced in their hearts," (cf. 2:37). because the Spirit changed the hearts of stone into hearts of flesh, as God promised us in Ezekiel. When the Holy Spirit enters the heart, it will pierce the heart and will change and transform the person.

**3:4   And we have such trust through Christ toward God.** Such

confidence! What is this trust? The trust is in our sufficiency. We have this trust that we are sufficient for this ministry, but this trust is through Christ, not through ourselves. This trust is also toward God—in our relationship to God as His ministers, as His servants." We have this trust that we are sufficient—sufficient to serve God and to be ministers of God. This sufficiency is through Christ, meaning that if Christ had not died on the Cross, if Christ had not saved us, if Christ had not sent the Holy Spirit—the Spirit of Grace—no one would be found sufficient.

**3:5   Not that we are sufficient of ourselves to think of anything as being from ourselves, but our sufficiency is from God.** No one can say "I am sufficient to be a servant"; if there is sufficiency, this sufficiency is from God through Christ Jesus, through His salvation and His sending of the Holy Spirit. "I cannot give any credit to myself for establishing the church in Corinth; my strength is from God."

**3:6   Who also made us sufficient as ministers of the new covenant.** He was saying, "God enabled us and empowered us to be ministers and servants of the New Covenant. The New Covenant is far more excellent than the Old Covenant." The Old Covenant was based on human effort, but the New

Covenant is based on the grace of God. Here, St. Paul was actually comparing himself to the Judaizer. The Judaizers wanted to be servants to the Old Covenant, they wanted to bring people back to the Law, to "salvation through the Law," salvation through human effort without Jesus Christ, without the Grace of God. But St. Paul was saying that we are servants of the New Covenant. This New Covenant established on the grace of God without human effort, the covenant of Christ. He starts, from this verse, to compare between the Old Covenant and the New Covenant. The Old Covenant had no grace in it—the Holy Spirit was not working in the lives of the people. They had the letters and the words, but there was no Spirit accompanying the Letter; this was a big difference. When you read any verse in the Scripture, you are not reading letters, but the Holy Spirit who inspired these words is actually accompanying every letter. It is the Holy Spirit who pierces your heart and who enables you to keep the Commandments. In the Old Testament, because salvation was not fulfilled, the Holy Spirit was not working within the people. We received the Holy Spirit only after salvation. Yes, the Holy Spirit was existent and working, but not to save the people. That is why the Lord said to the disciples, "Do not depart from Jerusalem until you receive power from on high"—the power of the Holy Spirit.

**not of the letter but of the Spirit.** In the Old Testament, the Commandment, "Love the Lord your God," was just letters, and you had the whole burden to keep this Commandment. No one was able to keep the Commandment, so everyone was under the curse and under the sentence of death, but in the New Covenant, this same Commandment, "Love the Lord your God," is not composed of mere letters; the Holy Spirit works through each letter, pierces your heart, enables you, and empowers you to be able to keep the Commandment.

**for the letter kills, but the Spirit gives life.** The letter kills. Why does the letter kill? Because if you do not keep the Commandment, you shall surely die. If the letter is without grace and without the Spirit, then no one can keep the Commandment.

The Spirit now works through the Letter, and empowers, enables, and gives me grace. This is why, now, I am able to keep the Commandment. And if I keep the Commandment, I will be alive."

**3:7  But if the ministry of death.** This refers to the Old Covenant. All the prophets ministered and served, but they died and went to hades, and their people also died and went to hades; no one was saved. Can you imagine, ministry and service, ministry and service, ministry and service, and at the end everyone goes to Hades? This is the ministry of death; there is no life in it.

**written and engraved on stones.**
This also refers to their hearts of stone,
because there was no grace of the Holy
Spirit.

**was glorious.** If the Old Covenant,
which was the ministry of death and
was written on stones had glory, how
much more excellent is the glory of the
New Covenant.

**so that the children of Israel could
not look steadily at the face of
Moses because of the glory of his
countenance, which glory was
passing away.** His second point is to
compare between the glory of the Old
Covenant and the glory of the New
Covenant. It is as if the glory of the Old
Covenant is like the glory of the moon,
but the glory of the New Covenant is
like the glory of the sun. "Yes, there
was glory," referring to Exodus 34:29.
When Moses descended from the
mountain, his face was shining, to the
extent that the people could not look at
the face of Moses, so Moses had to put a
veil on his face. It is like the light of the
moon, "once the sun shines, this moon
light totally disappears." In the same
way, the glory of the Old Covenant
totally disappeared when Christ rose on
us with His brightening glory.

**3:8 How will the ministry of the
Spirit not be more glorious.** The Old
Covenant is the "Letter," and the New
Covenant is the "Spirit." The glory of
the New Covenant is more excellent
than the glory of the Old Covenant.
How will the ministry of the Spirit not
be more glorious in the future? "The
ministry of the Gospel has glory now,
but it will have a fuller glory at the
second coming of Christ."

**3:9 For if the ministry of
condemnation had glory, the
ministry of righteousness exceeds
much more in glory.** I want you to keep
in mind the ways he described the Old
Covenant: (1) "Letter," (2) "ministry
of death," (3) "written on stones," (4)
"ministry of condemnation."—"do this
and you shall live, but if you do not
do it, you will be under the curse, you
will be condemned," but in the New
Covenant, because we have the Holy
Spirit in us, we have the grace of God
working in us and we are able to keep
the Commandment of God. Because
we can keep the Commandment of
God, we are righteous. That is why he
called the ministry of the Old Covenant
the "ministry of condemnation." And
the ministry of the New Covenant, the
"ministry of righteousness," because
now we are righteous in the Lord Jesus
Christ, through the Holy Spirit. Why
do we put white clothes on a child after
we baptize him? To say, he is righteous
through the blood of the Lord Jesus
Christ. It was as if he was saying to the
Corinthians, "What's wrong with you?

After you have now enjoyed the ministry of righteousness and of the Spirit—after God transformed your hearts to be hearts of flesh not hearts of stone, after you are now living by the Spirit and not by the Letter—Why do you want to go back to the Old Covenant, to salvation by the Old Covenant, by human effort without the grace of God? You are going to a lesser glory because if the ministry of condemnation had glory, the ministry of righteousness exceeds much more in glory"; The First Covenant condemned the people, the Second Covenant justified the people.

**3:10    For even what was made glorious had no glory in this respect, because of the glory that excels.** If you compare the glory of the Old Covenant with the excellent glory of the New Covenant then it is no glory. "The Old Covenant is as the glory of the moon and stars as it fades away before the glory in the sun, the exceeding glory of the Gospel of the New Covenant. This glory is temporary and totally disappeared after Christ came with grace and truth."

**3:11    For if what is passing away was glorious, what remains is much more glorious.** A message to the Judaizing teachers is clearly asserted here: the Old Covenant, the ministry of death—written and engraved on stones—is done away. No one may be saved by his own works without Christ or the grace of God; we are not under the Law but under grace. "What remains" refers to the New Covenant, which remains glorious.

**3:12    Therefore, since we have such hope, we use great boldness of speech.** We have hope and confidence that we are ministers of the New Covenant whose glory is far above and beyond the glory of the Old Covenant. Seeing then that we have such hope of the future glory that we will be glorified in heaven, we use great boldness of speech. With such a hope we declare the Gospel truth, boldly and without any reservation.

**3:13    Unlike Moses, who put a veil over his face so that the children of Israel could not look steadily.** "Now we have boldness; the glory is revealed, so we are speaking with open face, while Moses was covering his face," Was it because God wanted to hide this glory from them, or was it because they could not look at Moses? Actually, it was because they could not look at Moses. It was not the intention of God, but their weakness that made them unable to look at Moses and to have to look at a veil. "If you believe in Christ, then the glory will be revealed to you and you will be able to see the glory of the New Covenant. But if you do not believe in Christ and you want to abide by the Jewish Law, in which salvation is based on human efforts—with the Law and no grace—then you will be looking through a veil and unable to see the glory of God. There will be a veil covering your understanding, your mind, and your heart, and you cannot see the end of what was passing away."

**at the end of what was passing away.** The Old Covenant was passing away. What is "the end of what was passing away?" "The end" means the goal. Where was the end of the Old Covenant? In Christ. "I am preaching Christ with boldness, with an open face, not like Moses who had a veil." The veil that Moses put over his face was used by St. Paul as a symbol to show that all was not made plain in the Law of Moses. Nothing was made clear in the Law of Moses, even the sacrifices. Christ is hidden in the Old Covenant. The brightness with which the face of Moses shone was passing away; this glory was passing away but the end was Christ, because the whole Mosaic Law tended to and terminated in the Lord Jesus Christ. But the Israelites had only a dim—a very, very weak—sight of Him of whom Moses spoke in a very covert manner. St. Paul was passing from the literal fact, which was that Moses had a veil, to the spiritual meaning. It was not just that his face was shining and people could not look at his face. No, Christ was hidden in the Old Covenant; there was a veil blinding the people

because there was no grace in the Old Covenant." The lack of grace in the Old Covenant was the veil that blinded the people, but now Christ came and gave us His grace, so the veil was taken away and we behold His glory, as is said in the Gospel of St. John.

**3:14** **But their minds were blinded.** If you do not believe in Christ like the Judaizers and want to be saved by human effort only, without the grace of God, you will be blinded.

**For until this day the same veil remains unlifted in the reading of the Old Testament.** You read about the sacrifices but you do not know that the sacrifices are a symbol of the Cross. You read the prophecy in Isaiah: "Behold, the Virgin will conceive and give birth to a Son," but you do not see that this prophecy is about Christ because the veil remains unlifted.

**because the veil is taken away in Christ..** If you believe in Christ, the veil will be taken away, but if you do not believe in Christ then you will be blind. This was what the Lord said to the scribes and Pharisees, "Your problem is that you are blind but you say, 'We see,' that is why your sin remains. But if you believe in Christ, He will remove the veil, then you will actually be able to see" (cf. John 9:41).

**3:15** **But even to this day, when Moses is read, a veil lies on their heart.** "Moses" is referring to the Law of Moses, the Old Testament. They read it in their synagogues but do not understand it. The trouble is in their heart; they are blinded by not accepting the grace of God.

**3:16** **Nevertheless when one turns to the Lord, the veil is taken away.** When one accepts and believes in Christ—when one turns to the Lord—the veil is taken away. When one turns to God with his heart and repents and believes in Him as Lord, God, and Savior, the veil of blindness will fall away so that he will see clearly. We have a nice story here. Before his faith, before he believed in Christ, St. Paul was blind, but after he was baptized and believed in Christ, scales fell from his eyes. Thus, it is as if in believing in Christ, you are baptized and move from darkness into light. That is why we call baptism "the mystery of the sacrament of enlightenment," because now the veil is taken away so that we can see and behold His glory. ✤ He told us that the New Covenant is Spirit and not Letter; the Holy Spirit accompanies every letter and gives power. "Turning to the Lord" means to enter into the New Covenant—the Covenant of the Spirit—and the ministry of righteousness

**3:17** **Now the Lord is the Spirit; and where the Spirit of the Lord is.** In your heart. You are the temple of God and the Holy Spirit abides in you.

**there is liberty.** In your heart there is liberty. When you turn to the Lord there will be freedom and liberty from the bondage of sin and the bondage of Satan in your heart. This means you will no longer be slaves to the Letter, but you will be free to serve God in the Spirit and to rejoice in Jesus Christ. As St. Paul told us, we did not receive the spirit of bondage, but the Spirit of sonship; he said, "You will be free to worship Christ, you will be free from the bondage of sin and the bondage of Satan, and you will also be free from the fear of death."

**3:18** **But we all.** This refers to us Christians, the believers who were baptized and who received the Holy Spirit in the sacrament of Chrismation; we all who received the Holy Spirit. In the Commandment that the clergy says to the parents and the godparents after baptism, he says to them, "Your children, the day in which they were born they were slaves, but now they are free."

**with unveiled face.** "We all," the Christians, the believers, are those who received the Holy Spirit, not like the Israelites who are looking through the veil that is on the face of Moses.

**beholding as in a mirror the glory of the Lord.** We behold the glory of the Lord in the mirror of the Bible, the mirror of the church, but this glory, will be seen more clearly in the second coming of Christ.

**are being transformed into the same image.** He said, "The more you stand before God, the more you look at His glory in the mirror—in the church in worship, in the Bible when you read—what will happen to you? You also will be transformed into the same image—from glory to glory. Who is doing this? The Spirit of grace, just as by the Spirit of the Lord. What is the difference between looking at a veil or a mirror? If the glory is behind a veil what are you going to see? Nothing. But if you look at a screen to see what is going on inside the altar, then here you are looking at a mirror, which is much, much clearer. Moreover, in heaven we will see Him with an open face. With an open, unveiled face, all we Christians are, beholding as in a mirror (the mirror is the Gospel, the church of Christ) the glory of the Lord, looking at the Lord Jesus Christ and beholding His New Covenant. And as we keep this in our hearts and minds and contemplate on this glory, then we will be transformed into the same image, the image of God. We will be like Him; Christ will be portrayed in us. To look at the Lord has a transforming power! If we look at Him, we will be like Him. When Moses stood before the Lord he shone with glory. In the same way, we will reflect the glory of Christ. That is why he told us, "You are the light of the world," because Christ will be shining through us to the world.

**From glory to glory, just as by the Spirit of the Lord.** We will actually be growing from one stage of glory to a higher stage of glory. This glory is the work of grace, the work of the Holy Spirit in us. If we look at the Lord, at the New Covenant, at the Gospel, and at the church, we will be like Him and will show forth His glory.

## Chapter 3 Questions

1. Who was St. Paul's "epistle of commendation"?

2. What instrument had St. Paul used to make the Corinthians an "epistle of Christ"? And upon what had he written?

3. Who made St. Paul sufficient as a minister?

4. Of what is the new covenant? And what does it give?

5. How is the old and new covenant described in verses 7-11?

6. What happens when one turns to the Lord?

7. What does one find in turning to the Lord?

8. What happens when we behold the Lord's glory with unveiled face?

# 4

## Chapter Outline

- The Light of Christ's Gospel (1-6)
- Cast Down but Unconquered (7-15)
- Seeing the Invisible (16-18)

**4:1  Therefore, since we have this ministry, as we have received mercy, we do not lose heart.** In this verse, St. Paul gave two reasons why he does not lose heart. "We have this ministry," the ministry of the Spirit of life, the ministry of glory. "This ministry that is based on the grace of God empowers me, encourages me, so that even in the midst of all this persecution and hardship, I do not lose heart." ❖ I hope that we, as servants, focus on the glory of the service, on the glory of this ministry that God entrusted us with, so that when we see some hardships or problems in our service we do not say, "I cannot take it anymore, I am quitting." St. Paul is saying, "We should not lose heart, because we have such a glorious ministry

**as we have received mercy.** I am not serving by my own talents. I am not serving by my own power, nor by the excellent words of wisdom of this world, but because of His mercy. This was why he said, "I was a persecutor, I was a blasphemer, and God had mercy

on me and chose me and appointed me to such ministry, so if I face persecution now I will not lose heart because I myself was a persecutor before, and God transformed me, so I will not lose heart. That is why I will preach the Gospel in boldness of speech, in boldness of action, in patience and suffering. I will endure all these troubles and these sufferings because we have such a glorious ministry, and we have received such mercy from God."

**4:2  But we have renounced the hidden things of shame.** St. Paul was saying, "I am not ashamed of this ministry." The servants of Christ must turn away from all deceitful practices or teaching. St. Paul said, "No, the Gospel of Christ is unveiled and it preaches the glorious message of salvation. This is why we have renounced the hidden things of shame. I am not ashamed to say that Christ was crucified or that God became man to save me. I am not ashamed of the message of salvation, so I will not hide it from people and deceive them in the hidden ways of shame." St. Paul was rebuking the false and deceitful teachers who were trying to bring the Corinthians under the old Jewish programs. Shame usually leads to hiding; when a person is ashamed of something, he will hide it. But St. Paul was saying, "I am not ashamed of this message, that is why I will not hide it. I do not hide the message of the Gospel, but with great boldness of speech—

by the dispensation of speech—I will preach the Gospel of Christ."

**Not walking in craftiness nor handling the word of God deceitfully, but by manifestation of the truth.** In other words, not being like the false teachers who perverted the word of God and added elements from the Jewish tradition to it, which were just symbols for the Gospel of Christ and they brought forth ideas about Christ. "No, we will not preach the word with craftiness, nor will we handle the word of God deceitfully, but by manifestation of the truth."

**commending ourselves to every man's conscience in the sight of God.** He is referring to the false teachers who cast doubts on the apostleship of St. Paul. That is why in Chapter 3, St. Paul started by telling them, "Do we need recommendation letters for you? Should I bring recommendation letters to tell you that I am an apostle of Christ?" And now in Chapter 4, he is saying, "What then is my recommendation letter?" "My recommendation letter is that I will preach to you the truth of the message of the Gospel of Christ. By "manifestation of the truth," by preaching the truth, I will commend myself as an apostle, and you will know that I am an apostle for the Gentiles called by God. Who will judge me? I am not asking carnal people to judge me, I am not asking false teachers to judge me, to determine whether or not I am an apostle, but we commend

ourselves to every man's conscience in the sight of God. Those who have their conscience inspired by the Holy Spirit and make their judgement in the sight of God will know that I am a true apostle of the Lord Jesus Christ. That is why, by the manifestation of the truth I am commending myself to you and to every man's conscience in the sight of God—not in the sight of men."

**4:3** **But even if our gospel is veiled, it is veiled to those who are perishing.** He is comparing between the veil that was in the Old Testament and the veil that is in the Gospel for those who are perishing. In the Old Covenant, God hid the message from the people; He was speaking to them indirectly, in symbols. In the New Testament God is not hiding the message; the message is unveiled. He revealed Himself to us clearly and openly as the Son of God, and the message of salvation is clear. If my eye is blinded, I will not be able to see the light of the sun. If someone cannot see the truth of the Gospel, It is not because God hid it, but because that person is blinded. I am blinded because I refuse to believe in Him and accept Him, and Satan has now blinded me completely in order not to see the light of the Gospel.

**4:4** **whose minds the god of this age.** "Who is the god of this world?"—

and here, god is with a small 'g'. The god or the prince of the world is Satan. As we read in John 12:31 and in Philippians 3:19, Satan is called the "prince of this world," or the "god of this world."

**has blinded, who do not believe.** Satan blinded the minds of those who refuse to believe. How does Satan blind? By his deceitfulness. Satan's power lies in his ability to deceive. If Satan lost his ability to deceive, he would be powerless. That is why we say in the Divine Liturgy, "And when we fell, through the deceit of the serpent." As Satan deceived Eve and Adam and blinded them from seeing the Commandment of God, in the same way Satan cast doubts in the hearts of the people; blinding their minds so that they would not see the light of the Gospel.

**lest the light of the gospel of the glory of Christ.** This Gospel reveals to us the glory of Christ—the glory of Him as our King, as our Savior, and as He who abolished the power of death.

**who is the image of God.** TAnd who is Christ? He is the image of God. No one has seen the Father, but if we see the Son, we see the Father—as the Lord said to Philip, "If you see me, you have seen the Father" (cf 14:9).

**should shine on them.** And why did Satan blind their minds? Lest the light of the Gospel of the glory of Christ should shine on them and they believe, so he blinded them completely.

**4:5    For we do not preach ourselves, but Christ Jesus the Lord.** The false teachers again attacked, so he answered this accusation saying, "When I told you to follow me, I was not saying 'I am your god, follow me, worship me;' No. I am saying, 'See how God had mercy on me and transferred me from the darkness of sin into the light of Christ. See how after I was a persecutor of the church I am now persecuted.' I am telling you to follow my footsteps as I am following the footsteps of Christ.

**and ourselves your bondservants for Jesus' sake.** I know I am your servant, your bondservant." The accurate translation of the word "bondservant" is slave. St. Paul is saying, "I am not saying that I am your god. In fact, I am saying that I am your slave for Christ's sake, to bring the Gospel of salvation to you. I am not preaching myself but I am preaching Christ as our Lord. We have no self-seeking here but we seek only to preach Jesus Christ."

**4:6    For it is the God who commanded light to shine out of darkness, who has shone in our hearts to give the light of the knowledge of the glory of God in the**

**face of Jesus Christ.** He told them, "I was living in darkness," comparing himself before his conversion with the description of the earth in Genesis 1:1, when the earth was void, formless, and there was darkness. What did God mean here in Genesis 1:3 when He said, "Let there be light?" At that time light actually started to shine on earth. St. Paul said, "As God made light shine in the darkness of the earth, in the same way, God shone His light in my heart. I was blind, I was walking in the darkness but now I see the light of Christ. That is why I want each one of you to taste and see the light of Christ." "I want you to know the height of the glory of the knowledge of God. When you know Christ, you will know the glory of God the Father, because the glory of God the Father is revealed to us in His Son, Jesus Christ, and this knowledge in itself is light; your knowledge enlightens your minds." He is saying, "As God enlightened my heart, I am calling you to believe in Christ so the light of the knowledge of the glory of God, in the face of Jesus Christ, may shine in your hearts." He is referring here to Genesis 1:3, how God brought light to the darkness of the earth and how in the same way, the glory of God is revealed in His Son who has shown us excellency, the tenderness of the Father and the love of God.

**4:7   But we have this treasure in earthen vessels.** This verse is in response to another accusation. The first accusation was that they cast doubt on his apostleship. The second accusation was: "Paul is preaching himself; he told you to follow him." The third accusation against St. Paul was, "See how many sufferings he is facing? If he is the apostle of God, God would save him from all these sufferings." St. Paul responds to that accusation, begging first by referring to himself as being an earth vessel (we are the earthly vessels—the ministers, servants, apostles. "I am the earthen vessel.") and the treasure carried in the earthen vessel is  the knowledge of Christ, the glorious ministry of the New Covenant. St. Paul goes on to respond to the accusation as follows:

**that the excellence of the power may be of God and not of us.** He was saying, "If we are strong having no persecutions or hardships and spread the Gospel of Christ, people may claim that the evangelism and preaching of the Gospel of Christ is because of our power—because we are wise and strong we are able to spread the Gospel of Christ. If people realize that we are weak and surrounded by suffering from all sides, yet in spite of this the Gospel of Christ is spreading everywhere and many people are believing in Christ and churches are growing, then here, "the excellence of the power may be of God and not of us." Here St. Paul wanted to say that as God sent the apostles saying "Take no money, take no clothes; do not rely on any earthly things and I will show you how you will spread the Gospel of Christ," so "the excellence of the power may be of God and not of us." The treasure of the knowledge of Christ, the ministry of the Gospel of Christ, the earthen vessels are the servants; this way, we can see how the word of God is attributed to His power, not to us.

**4:8 We are hard-pressed on every side, yet not crushed.** From every side we are troubled and hard-pressed; We are pressured, yet not crushed. That is the excellence of the power of God. You expect that if we are troubled from every side and people are pressuring us from every side, putting restrictions and pressuring us, we would be crushed. But the result is that we are not crushed—that is the excellent power of God.

**we are perplexed, but not in despair.** We are perplexed because of persecution, suffering, and hardships. Many times, we are confused. Many times we say, "Where is God?" But in spite of all this we never fall into despair. Yes, we face overwhelming difficulties every day, but the God of hope is with us, so we never fall into despair. Our frailty of the earthen vessel is that we are perplexed, but the excellence of the power of God is that we are not in despair.

**4:9 Persecuted, but not forsaken.** Persecuted, yes, but not forsaken. God promised us, "I will never leave you nor forsake you." Yes we are persecuted. Every day we face persecution by our enemies, but God never forsakes us and constantly gives us victory and prosperity.

**struck down, but not destroyed.** What do you expect if one is struck down? To be destroyed. But no, although we are struck down, we are not destroyed. We are overthrown and cast to the earth but God empowers us and makes us stand again and we are never destroyed. The church of God is strong in spite of all the persecution and attacks against it because God holds us, that the gates of hades shall not prevail against it. St. Paul, in verses 8 and 9, in a wonderful and amazing way, explained how we have this treasure in earthly vessels. Treasure—the treasure that we are not destroyed, not in despair, not distressed, not forsaken, but rather in earthly vessels—those who are troubled, perplexed, persecuted, cast down, or struck down.

**4:10 Always carrying about in the body the dying of the Lord Jesus.** He continues here his explanation about the earthy vessels or the weak vessels, and the excellence of the power of God. We are frequently facing sufferings, persecutions, and threats of death as the Lord Jesus Christ did

**That the life of Jesus also may be manifested in our body.** St. Paul was stoned, he faced death several times, he was shipwrecked more than once, he was scourged more than once—and despite all of these "dyings" of Christ, he was still alive. God upheld him and so he said, "In this life, according to the rules of human mortality, I should be dead, but the life I am living right now is the life of Christ manifested in me. I want to share this life so that you may enjoy the life of Christ; I am facing death every day so that you may experience the life of salvation. We die daily for Christ so that you may live for Him, when you say, 'How is St. Paul still alive despite all the suffering and persecution?'"

**4:11** **For we who live are always delivered to death for Jesus' sake, that the life of Jesus also may be manifested in our mortal flesh.** We, whom you are seeing alive are always delivered to death for Jesus' sake. Why have I accepted this? That the life of Jesus also may be manifested in our mortal flesh." St. Paul was saying, "The ministers, servants, and apostles of Christ are always exposed to death and risk their lives in order to preach life to others." He was saying, "The fact that God preserved me in the middle of all these 'dyings' actually means that God can give you life, and can move you from death to the death of sin, and into the life of salvation."

**4:12** **So then death is working in us, but life in you.** Every day, I am exposed to death, because that is the only way to reach the life of salvation here. I am exposed to death that you may enjoy the life of salvation. And the life that you witness in me—in my mortal body –will daily bear witness that Christ can give you the same life; a life of salvation.

**4:13** **And since we have the same spirit of faith.** Many people may start to question, "How can you endure all these sufferings? How do you not lose hope?" In the beginning of the chapter St. Paul gave us two reasons: "God had mercy on us, and we have such a glorious service." Then he gave us more reasons why we should not lose hope amid all the suffering, amid all tribulations.

**according to what is written, "I believed and therefore I spoke," we also believe and therefore speak.** A third reason why you should not lose hope is because of the faith. "According to what is written, 'I believed and therefore I spoke,' we also believe and therefore speak." St. Paul was referring to Psalm 116:10. In this Psalm David said, "I believe and therefore I spoke," so St. Paul was saying, "Preaching the Gospel is based on our faith, and we have the same Spirit—the Spirit St. David had—the Spirit of faith. This faith in Christ compelled me to preach the Gospel of salvation to you, and encouraged me to endure all these sufferings, especially now that the faith is more open and is not veiled like the Old Covenant. We know we will be risen, so even if we are killed, we will rise again because Jesus Christ rose from the dead."

**4:14    Knowing that He who raised up the Lord Jesus will also raise us up with Jesus, and will present us with you.** "All they can do is kill the body, they cannot do anything more than this; they cannot kill the Spirit. Even the body that they can kill, God will raise in the last day—in the second coming—as Jesus rose from the dead. As Jesus rose from the dead, in the same way we will be raised in the second coming of Christ. That is why we do not lose heart. This is our faith: if we die for Him, He will raise us. This is why we preach. We are not afraid. We will preach even if they are going to kill us, because they cannot do more than this. Even if they kill us, God will raise us again in the last day.

**4:15   For all things are for your sakes, that grace, having spread through the many, may cause thanksgiving to abound to the glory of God.** Again St. Paul is telling them, "I am not preaching of myself. If I were preaching of myself, I would not face

all these threats and sufferings day after day. I am accepting all this for you. All things are for your sakes—our suffering, our daily dying, I am accepting all this for you that the grace of God—the New Covenant—when It spreads through many, and many believe in Christ, would cause thanksgiving. People will give thanks to God, and thanksgiving will abound to the glory of God. My ultimate goal is to glorify God. I am accepting death for your sake, that you may accept the grace of God."

**4:16    Therefore we do not lose heart. Even though our outward man is perishing, yet the inward man is being renewed day by day.** Yes, our outward man, our body, is perishing—from suffering and hardships, but our spirit is renewed every day, like youth, "He will renew your youth like an eagle" (cf. Isaiah 40:30-31). He was saying, "Though our body wastes away under trials and we are threatened with death, yet our spirit is renewed day by day, our spiritual strength is constantly renewed by Christ.

**4:17    For our light affliction, which is but for a moment, is working for us a far more exceeding and eternal weight of glory.** I want you to see the contrast here. He used the word "light" contrasted by the word "weight"; and he used "affliction" and the contrast is "glory"; and he used "for a moment" and the contrast here is "exceeding and eternal." He was saying, "Our affliction is light and for a moment, but our glory is heavy and eternal." Although St. Paul faced many afflictions, he held them lightly. His eyes were focused on the glorious reward that he would receive. Although he faced continuous suffering he said, "We die daily for Christ but we consider this suffering but for a moment." He kept his mind on the eternal life. ❖ This is a lesson for all of us. If you focus on earthly suffering, it seems heavy and as if it will last forever. But if you see suffering in the light of eternal glory, you will see that suffering is nothing. It is actually very light and for a moment, but the glory is heavy, weighty, and eternal. In this way, you will not lose heart; you will easily put up with sufferings and hardships if you always look to the eternal glory. The Cross will be light if we see the resurrection and the eternal crown. The sorrow that we endure for Christ, prepares for us eternal glory. That is a fifth reason why we should endure suffering.

**4:18  While we do not look at the things which are seen, but at the things which are not seen.** The suffering is what is seen, but the glory is what is not seen.

**For the things which are seen are temporary, but the things which are not seen are eternal.** Where are your eyes fixed? If your eyes are fixed on the unseen—on the eternal glory—then your physical eyes cannot behold the affliction. In fact, it will be easy for you to endure affliction, persecution, and suffering for Christ, and you will actually long for this eternal glory. Whatever is seen is temporary, whether pleasures, riches, sufferings, or hardships of the world; the world will pass away and all its glory. Whatever is seen is perishable and temporary, even this earth and this heaven; this heaven and earth are passing away, but God's heaven, the eternal life, the glory, the crowns which we cannot see right now, these are eternal. That is why we should let our eyes turn to the unseen rather than seeing the things that are seen, this will empower us to endure the suffering and not lose heart in the midst of sufferings.

## Chapter 4 Questions

1. In verse 3, to whom the gospel is veiled?

2. In verse 7, "But we have this treasure in earthen vessels", what is meant by treasure and earthen vessels?

3. In verse 11, "For we who live are always delivered to death for Jesus," explain why.

4. In verse 16, "Therefore we do not lose heart. Though outwardly we are wasting away, yet inwardly we are being renewed day by day." Compare between the outwardly man and inwardly man.

5. In verse 16, why we should not lose heart?

# 5

requirements like this earthly body, that is why St. Paul called it a heavenly and eternal body

## Chapter Outline

**5:1 For we know that if our earthly house, this tent, is destroyed.** Keeping in mind the words of Christ, St. Paul said, "This body is a tent, a temporary, earthly house, in which we are camping during a journey. And even if they kill me, even if I die and the body be dissolved, this is not the end of the story, because if our earthly house is destroyed, we have a building from God."

**we have a building from God, a house not made with hands, eternal in the heavens.** What is this building from God? He is speaking about the glorified body—"We have a building from God, a house not made with hands"—not with earthly hands, but "eternal in the heavens." We read in 1 Corinthians 15 how St. Paul spoke about the resurrection of the bodies, and in the Creed before baptism, the baptized person says, "I believe in the resurrection of the bodies." These bodies will be raised, but in a glorified way. It will be a spiritual body—meaning, the body will not have physiological

**5:2 For in this we groan, earnestly desiring to be clothed with our habitation which is from heaven.** "While we are in this weak body—in this tent—we groan and suffer. This is why we long for deliverance from this body. Once we die and are raised with Christ there is no suffering nor pain anymore. That is why we long for deliverance from this body and for the eternal, spiritual, glorified bodies. In this body we groan and suffer. That is why we earnestly desire to be clothed, to put on the spiritual, glorified body of resurrection, which is heaven." When the spirit leaves this body, it is as if leaving old and worn out clothing. In the second coming of Christ and at the resurrection of the dead we will be clothed with a heavenly body. In Greece — because Corinth is a city in Greece — there was a theory that when the person dies and the spirit leaves the mortal body, then it remains without a body eternally. In other words, they do not believe in the resurrection of the bodies. They say the body will return to dust and that is it. St. Paul here is emphasizing the truth of the resurrection of the body.

**5:3** **If indeed, having been clothed, we shall not be found naked.** If we will put on the heavenly body, then we shall not be found naked; the spirit will not be without a body. "If the spirit is without a body, it is naked. But when we put on a body—the glorified body—then we are clothed, we are not naked." Verse 3 is one of the verses that support the resurrection of the body.

**5:4** **For we who are in this tent groan, being burdened, not because we want to be unclothed, but further clothed, that mortality may be swallowed up by life.** In this earthly body, while we are here on earth, we groan, we suffer. "Being burdened" with the sufferings and the hardships that we face every day. But here, St. Paul emphasized, "Not that we want to be unclothed." St. Paul intended by this, "It is not our wish to be without bodies, but our desire is to be clothed with the heavenly body." When we put on the eternal, glorified body— the heavenly and spiritual body—then this mortality, this mortal body, will be swallowed up by life. It is not our wish to be free from a body, but our desire is to have a better one. We wish to lay off the mortal garment and to be further clothed with the heavenly garment, the spiritual body which is immortal and eternal

**5:5** **Now He who has prepared us for this very thing is God.** He was saying, "God from the very beginning created man from body and spirit, so it is God's plan for us to have a spirit and a body." That is why, in the second coming of Christ, we will be spirit and bodies. When death entered into the world by the envy of the devil, we acquired this desire for immortality; God is the One who placed in us the desire for immortality.

**who also has given us the Spirit as a guarantee.** God died to abolish the power of death, and He rose in order to give us the power of life, to be raised with Him in His second coming. If the Spirit raised Jesus Christ from death and then God gave us the Holy Spirit to dwell in us, why did God give It to us? As a guarantee, that if you have the Spirit of God, you will be raised—that is what St. Paul said. God put in us the longing for immortality; who also gave us the Holy Spirit as a guarantee, as a proof of fulfillment of His promise that when He comes again, He will raise us with Him and we will live eternally with Him.

**5:6** **So we are always confident.** We are confident in the resurrection of the bodies, confident that in the second coming of Christ we will be raised, confident that we will inherit with Him the Kingdom of Heaven. Who gave us this confidence? The Holy Spirit who abides in us.

**knowing that while we are at home in the body, we are absent from the Lord.** He called it "home, earthly home"—"we are absent from the Lord." Does this mean that "we are absent from the Lord?" We do not see Him by sight, but we see Him by faith, so therefore we are absent from Him. This makes us long to see Him by sight. Every one of us wants to see Christ with his very own eyes, that is why we have the desire to depart from this world, to be with Christ, to see Him face to face.

**5:7 For we walk by faith, not by sight.** That is why he said, "We are absent; we see God by the eyes of faith but not by sight."

**5:8 We are confident, yes, well pleased rather to be absent from the body and to be present with the Lord.** When we die and go to heaven, we will be raised with Christ, will see Him, and will be present with the Lord. That is why we are not only longing for this but we are well pleased. We desire to depart from the body to be with Christ. This is our happiness and our pleasure—to be with Him always. That is why the departure of the saints is considered a feast—because this is the wedding day in which our souls will be wed to Christ. Knowing that we will be raised, knowing that we will go to heaven.

**5:9 Therefore we make it our aim, whether present or absent, to be well pleasing to Him.** Just as the ten virgins who went with the Bridegroom were the ones who were ready and wise, so too we strive to live in a way that both in our life here we may please Him, and at His second coming we may be found pleasing to Him. That is why he said, "Whether present or absent, to be well pleasing to Him." He is reminding us that in the second coming of the Lord, He will judge everyone according to his deeds, whether good or evil. That is why we need to strive to be well pleasing to Him.

**5:10 For we must all appear before the judgment seat of Christ, that each one may receive the things done in the body, according to what he has done, whether good or bad.** Remembering that we will stand before the judgement seat of Christ will stimulate you to strive to be pleasing to Him. The objective of the judgement is that we may reap the fruit of what we have done in the body, whether good or bad; we will be given according to our deeds.

**5:11** **Knowing, therefore, the terror of the Lord, we persuade men.** Fear God because you will give an account before Him, and use the fear of God to live a righteous life. The fear of the Lord, the terror of the Lord made St. Paul faithful and honest in his ministry and as he said, "Knowing, therefore, the terror of the Lord, we persuade men"—we persuade men to please God. He told them, "You will stand before God, you will give an account, so keep the fear of the Lord in your heart and live righteously and please Him. Do His will and seek His acceptance."

**but we are well known to God, and I also trust are well known in your consciences.** St. Paul began to respond to the false accusations by the false teachers that he was not an apostle, was seeking his own glory and was asking people to follow him. He said, "We are well known to God. God sees our whole life, God sees our faithfulness. Our faithfulness in ministry to persuade men is motivated not by the fear of men, but by the fear of God. God sees our whole life and knows the motives of our ministry, and also knows our deeds." St. Paul continued, "Just as God knows us very well, I hope that you at Corinth know me. I want to have a witness in your conscience, to know that I am faithfully serving the Lord because I fear Him, not because I seek my own glory."

**5:12** **For we do not commend ourselves again to you, but give you opportunity to boast on our behalf, that you may have an answer for those who boast in appearance and not in heart.** St. Paul was saying, "I do not want to praise myself, defend myself or my ministry, but actually 'I want to give you an opportunity to boast on our behalf, that you may have an answer for those who boast in appearance and not in heart.'" St. Paul was telling them, "I do not want to commend myself anymore to you. But when I am speaking about the fear of God, of how I am faithful in my ministry and motivated by the fear of the Lord, I am actually giving you opportunity to defend us and to glorify God over our work and our life, so that you can answer the false teachers who attack me — not to defend me, but to defend your faith, because they are casting doubt on your faith." He was saying, "I am now giving you an opportunity — by examining my service, my teaching, and my preaching — to be able to give an answer to the false teachers who teach you to boast in appearances, to boast from the outside, the external circumcision, not by the internal circumcision of the heart through baptism and putting off the old man and putting on the new man."

**5:13** **For if we are beside ourselves, it is for God.** He was saying, "If it is true that we have lost our minds (as we are accused) then

God understands the emotions, which God gave us, and inspired us with, to defend the faith. These emotions that you describe as madness and craziness, God understands very well and it is He who gave us these emotions. This is for God, that we defend the faith and spread the good news of the Gospel."

**or if we are of sound mind, it is for you.** "Despite the fact that you believe that we are beside ourselves and have lost our minds (we have not) these emotions that seem as madness to you are to defend the Gospel; they are for God. But if you see us at other times as being of sound mind, it is in order to reason with you, persuade you, and to preach to you the word of salvation. If we are of sound mind, it is for you."

**5:14** **For the love of Christ compels us.** As St. Paul said, "We are motivated by the fear of God." Now he was giving another reason: we are not only motivated by the fear of God, but also by the love of Christ. It was the love of Christ that moved him in all his conduct, whether to appear as crazy and having lost his mind, or to appear as with a sound mind. The love of Christ is compelling, constraining, and this love appeared in the death of Christ on the Cross. And why did He die? He died on the Cross because He wants us to die with Him to sin, and to rise with Him a new creation. St. Paul was saying, "I, who was a blasphemer, a persecutor

of the Church of God, am now a new creation and I know that I am a new creation because Christ loved me, died for me, transformed me, delivered me from the sinful life I was living, and He gave me a new life."

**because we judge thus: that if One died for all, then all died.** If Christ died for all, for everybody, then all died in Him. Whoever accepts Him dies in Him; that is what we have in baptism— we die with Christ.

**5:15** **And He died for all, that those who live should live no longer for themselves, but for Him who died for them and rose again.** The life that we have right now is not actually ours; the wages of sin is death. Because of our sins, all of us should die, so if we are alive now, this life is not ours. This life is a gift from Christ to us; He gave it to us because He loved us. Because of this love, this life which is not ours, we will not live according to our own desires, but we will live it according to Him.    we are dead, because of our sins—"but for Him," because our life now is His life, "who died for them and rose again." ❈ In baptism we die with Him; Christ died in order to give us life so that we should not live for ourselves anymore, but for Christ who died for us. That is exactly what St. Paul did. After his transformation he consecrated his life to the ministry, he consecrated his life to Christ.

**5:16** **Therefore, from now on, we regard no one according to the flesh. Even though we have known Christ according to the flesh, yet now we know Him thus no longer.** As all have died so as to live new lives for Christ, so now they are not to be known as belonging to the old fleshy race, but as members in Christ's body. I cannot say I am Jewish, or I am Greek; in Christ there is no Jew or Greek, but we are all one in His body. That is why he said, "From now on, after we die and rise with Christ, we regard no one according to the flesh." I do not say that Jews are the chosen people of God nor do I regard a certain race or certain nation, but all are the same in Christ. There is no difference between male and female, there is no difference between Jews and Gentiles, there is no difference between black and white; in Christ we are all the same, even those who boast that they met Christ in the flesh—because at the time that St. Paul wrote this Letter, some people who had actually seen Christ in the flesh were still living. St. Paul is saying, "Even though we have known Christ according to the flesh, yet now we know Him thus no longer." ❖ Most of the people who knew Christ according to the flesh followed Him for the healing of their sickness, to feed their hunger. The Lord told them in John 6:27, "You follow Me not because you saw wonders, but because you ate of the bread and were filled. Labor not for the food that perishes, but labor for the Food that does not perish." This is why St. Paul said, "Even Christ—we should not know Him by the flesh, but we should know Him by the Spirit." What does that mean? Knowing Christ by the flesh means to love Him with emotional, not spiritual, love, to boast that you talked with Him in the flesh, expect temporal benefits from Him, heal your diseases, provide food for you, and give you earthly and temporal blessings. But St. Paul said, "No, our goal now is not to know Christ according to the flesh, which means to ask earthly desires and blessings from Him, but to know Him spiritually—as new creatures—and we long for our spiritual, eternal life, not for the earthly things that will pass away."

**5:17** **Therefore, if anyone is in Christ, he is a new creation.** That is, a spiritual creation, not an earthly one.

**old things have passed away; behold, all things have become new.** We are new creatures because we died with Christ. We were buried with Him in baptism and we are risen to walk in a new life. The old life with all its passions, desires, and sins ended in baptism—when we died and were buried. The affections, motives, thoughts, and hopes of the old life, even the whole life has changed; now it is new in Christ.

**5:18  Now all things are of God.**
Usually, when St. Paul used the word
"God," he was referring to the Father.
So when he said, "All things are of
God" he was saying, "The salvation
that Christ fulfilled, the new life that
we received in baptism, everything was
according to the will of the Father," as
we say in the praises, "According to the
will of the Father and the pleasure of the
Son and the Holy Spirit, He was born
and saved us." Therefore, "All things
are of God" means, it is the Father who
planned all of this according to His will.

**who has reconciled us to Himself
through Jesus Christ.** The Father
is the One who sent Christ, His only
begotten Son to the world to reconcile
us to Him. Because of our sins, we
were enemies, but when Christ died and
redeemed us, now we are reconciled
with the Father, through Jesus Christ.
Through the salvation that the Lord
fulfilled on the Cross, we have been
brought back to the love of God, to love
His will and follow and obey Him.

**and has given us the ministry of
reconciliation.** God reconciled us
in Jesus Christ, then He appointed
ministers, servants, apostles, priests,
and bishops in the church. The
objective of our service is to call
people to be reconciled with God, to
accept the sacrifice of Christ and to
repent and be reconciled with God, to
be transformed and to be at peace with
God.  ❖  The new priest is ordained
after the reconciliation prayer, before
the deacon says, "Greet one another
with a holy kiss," because the priest is a
servant of reconciliation, is performing
the ministry of reconciliation. He is
asking the people, on behalf of God, to
be reconciled with God.

**5:19  that is, that God was in Christ
reconciling the world to Himself,
not imputing their trespasses to
them, and has committed to us the
word of reconciliation.** In Christ,
we are offered peace by forgiveness
of our sins, and we were shown the
love of God. How did God reconcile
us to Himself? By making Christ a sin
sacrifice—He is the Lamb of God who
takes away the sin of the whole world.
He imputed our trespasses and so we
became righteous in Christ—now we
can be reconciled to the Father. He gave
us the "word of reconciliation," what is
the word of reconciliation? The word
of reconciliation is to persuade men to
accept God's love and mercy for them
and to repent, so that God may forgive
their trespasses. As Peter, on the Day of
Pentecost said to the people, "Repent
and be baptized"—that is the word of
reconciliation. We have the message of
God, that is why St. Paul said, "We are
the ambassadors for Christ."

**5:20** **Now then, we are ambassadors for Christ, as though God were pleading through us: we implore you on Christ's behalf, be reconciled to God.** The servant, the priest, the clergy, and the bishop should understand that he is the ambassador of Christ. An ambassador does not preach his own message, but the message of God. We are His authorized messengers, speaking for God, beseeching the people for Christ, and in His name to be reconciled to God by repentance and by the obedience of faith. It is as if God is speaking to the world through the clergy, through His servants. The pastors are saying, "We implore you on Christ's behalf, be reconciled to God," be reconciled to God by repentance and by accepting the faith.

**5:21** **For He made Him who knew no sin to be sin for us.** "He" the Father, made "Him" the Son, who knew no sin, to be sin. Why? For us. How did He make Him sin? Because He carried our sins. He is the Lamb of God who carried the sin of the whole world. As a sinless Redeemer He carried our sins, and He was made sin to atone for us. He became a sin offering and a trespass offering to forgive our sins.

**that we might become the righteousness of God in Him.** The reason "He made Him who knew no sin to be sin for us" is so that our sins might thus be atoned for, that the Law would be satisfied, and so we would be forgiven. So now we have the righteousness of God in Christ, now we become righteous in Christ, since we die with Christ, in Christ we are justified and we became righteous.

---

## Chapter 5 Questions

1. St. Paul gives us two analogies for our earthly body. What are they? What are the similarities between the flesh and these two?

2. What is the real motive for St Paul to desire clothing with the heavenly clothes?

3. What will happen to our earthly body in the second coming of Christ?

4. "God gave us the Spirit as a guarantee." A guarantee for what? How is the Spirit being a guarantee?

5. Reconciliation is a great deed. Who did it? Why Him? How did He make it?

6. "For we walk by the faith." How does our faith in Eternal life affect our concept towards the flesh? How do you apply this in your daily life?

7. "The love of Christ compel us" (or controls us) (v.14). Do you think it is an advantage or disadvantage to be surrounded by Christ's love? Explain.

8. "If anyone is in Christ, he is a new creation" (v.17). In what ways we should be a new creation?

9. "He has given us the ministry of reconciliation" Do you feel responsible for this ministry? What do you do to be a good ambassador for Christ?

## Chapter Outline

• Marks of the Ministry (1-10)
• Be Holy (11-18)

it in vain; make use of it. God gave you His grace to help you to be saved, so do not just put it away and do not fall away from the grace of God. Especially since the time now is the time of salvation, the time of visitation, the time of redemption.

**6:1 We then, as workers together with Him also plead with you not to receive the grace of God in vain.** In other words, "St. Paul and Timothy and I, who, working together composed this letter, are also working with Christ. 'Also plead with you'—on behalf of Christ, as ambassadors who are pleading with you—'not to receive the grace of God in vain.'" You received the grace of God. What is the grace of God? It is the grace of the Holy Spirit that is received in baptism and in Chrismation. The Holy Spirit works in us the grace of sonship, the grace of salvation, the work of God, the church, the ministry of reconciliation, the sacraments of the church—all these are the grace of God that we received in order to be saved. St. Paul, as an ambassador of Christ, was pleading with them, begging them, asking them not to receive it in vain. To receive it in vain means that after you receive the grace of God, you despise it, let it fall away, put it off, not stir it up in your heart, not let the grace of God lead you and direct you. That is why he was telling them, "You have received the grace of God, please do not receive

**6:2 For He says.** "He," being God, is who is speaking in Isaiah 49:8, which is the prophecy St. Pual is referencing. This prophecy actually speaks about the power of salvation to the Gentiles. Starting from Isaiah Chapter 40 to the end of the book, Isaiah prophesied about the time of grace, the time of salvation, the acceptance of the Gentiles—the non-Jewish people—into salvation. Corinth, a Gentile city, was not Jewish.

**"In an acceptable time I have heard you, And in the day of salvation I have helped you."** This is the time of the New Covenant, the time in which the Son of God became man in order to redeem us and to save the Gentiles; this is the acceptable time, the day of salvation—salvation for all the people, including the Gentiles. Do not receive the grace of God in vain, the grace of salvation that was given to you, that you may actually receive it.

**Behold, now is the accepted time; behold, now is the day of salvation.** St. Paul is putting an emphasis on "now," because now is all we can control. You cannot control the past and there is no guarantee in the future; all you can control is now. We do not know if we are going to live until tomorrow. God is calling you now, God is asking you now to receive His grace, so now is the acceptable time, now is the time of salvation. Do not harden your heart; open your heart and accept the grace of God.

**6:3 We give no offense in anything, that our ministry may not be blamed.** There is a big lesson for us here, especially for servants: it does not matter what your gifts are and what your talents are,—in fact, those in the church of Corinth had many, many gifts—but if there is no confidence in the purity and holiness of the servant, then he will be ineffective. If you have many talents but you are offending people because you are not careful to live a life of holiness, a life of purity, then your ministry will actually be of no effect. That is why every servant should be anxious that his life does not hinder the Gospel of Christ. When people listen to the word of the Gospel from us, they also look at our conduct and behavior, and if we are offending the people with our life then our message will be weak and not influential.

**6:4 But in all things we commend ourselves as ministers of God.** It is as if he is saying, "We recommend

ourselves to you, we demonstrated ourselves to you, we presented ourselves to you as faithful and sincere ministers and servants of God." How? In patience. In the book of Sirach 2:1 we read, "My son, if you come to serve the Lord, prepare yourself for many tribulations." In accepting God you need to be ready to face any tribulations. How should you conduct yourself during these tribulations? You need to be patient. But if you start to lose your temper, if you start to be angry, if you start to be impatient, then you are actually giving offense in the ministry, and perhaps the ministry will be blamed and the Gospel of Christ will be hindered. That is why, as servants, you need to be patient.

**in much patience, in tribulations, in needs, in distresses.** When we face tribulations, how do we cope with these tribulations? By patience and endurance. When we suffer need, when we are lacking, what do we do? We become patient, we do not lose our temper, we do not become restless. But even if we suffer need, as St. Paul said in Philippians Chapter 4, "I learned how to be hungry and how to be full, how to be abased and how to abound"—you need to demonstrate patience in tribulation, in need, in distress. Yes, there are many stressors. Many times the servant is stressed by the many demands of the people, the many demands of the service, but how should you react to these stressors? If you lose your temper, you become angry, you become impatient, you are offending the ministry, you are causing the ministry to be blamed, you are hindering the Gospel of Christ.

### 6:5 in stripes, in imprisonments.

In 2 Corinthians Chapter 11 St. Paul said that five times he was scourged 39 whips—to that extent he endured the stripes. He also endured being imprisoned. He was left in prison several times, at least in Philippi (Acts 16:24), in Jerusalem (Acts 22:24), in Caesarea (Acts 24:23), and in Rome (Acts 28:16). Many times he was imprisoned but he was patient, he endured, and accepted.

**in tumults.** Tumults means attacks that the regular man cannot endure, but St. Paul, through the grace of God, was strong enough to withstand these attacks. That is why he told them, "Please, do not receive the grace of God in vain, you need it. You need the grace of God when you are subject to complete attacks. The grace of God will help you to be patient."

**in labors.** I\As St. Paul said in Acts, "I worked by my own hand to spread the Gospel of Christ throughout all the countries, at no charge." So actually, in spite of preaching the Gospel, he was working with his hand in order to support his ministry financially, and to also support those who were serving with him—in *labor*.

**in sleeplessness.** He spent many nights without sleep or rest — in travels, in crowds of people, in preaching the Gospel of Christ — "and I did this with conviction, with no complaints; I did not complain because I spent so many nights without sleep.

**in fastings.** Fasting here is partly through the want of food, because as he said in Philippians Chapter 4, "I learned to be hungry." Many times he did not have food, which is why he needed to fast, and other times he fasted voluntarily, to support his ministry and ask the grace of God to help him, to develop self-control. As he said, "I discipline my body and bring it to subjection, lest after I preach to others, I myself am rejected." St. Paul in verse 5 actually gave them different examples of how in patience he endured tribulations, he endured needs, and he also endured distresses—in enduring stripes, imprisonments, tumults, labors, sleeplessness, and fastings

### 6:6 In verse 6 he gives the virtues, the fruit of the Holy Spirit in him and portrays how he lived and conducted himself as a servant of God.

**by purity.** The servant should be pure and holy in order to be a pure vessel of the Holy Spirit. Purity means simplicity from temptation, a chaste life, a holy life. We conduct ourselves by purity.

**by knowledge.** The servant of God should be knowledgeable of the Divine Scripture and of the Divine mysteries. How do you preach the word of God without being knowledgeable? How do you preach the word of God without knowing the word of God? So, he said, "By purity, by knowledge.

**by longsuffering.** Servants of God are expected to be longsuffering in all occasions, by being patient with people until they accept the faith, by enduring those who argue with us until they are convinced; longsuffering from place to place and preaching the word of God.

**by kindness.** St. Paul can be thought to say here, "I showed kindness even to the powerful persecutors; I was kind with them, I did not show harshness. I did not show cruelty, but I was kind."

**by the Holy Spirit.** "I was filled with the Holy Spirit. I allowed the Holy Spirit to actually bear fruits in me, I showed forth the Spirit's influence and power." As he said in 1 Corinthians 2, "When I came to you, I did not come with the excellence of speech or with human wisdom, but I came with the power and demonstration of the Sprit. I showed you that all the virtues I have are the work of the Holy Spirit in me. I did not hinder the work of the Holy Spirit in me."

**by sincere love.** That is, love without hypocrisy. Showing unconditional love, limitless love to everybody, sacrificial love, a wealth of love to all, because love is a fruit of the Spirit, as we read in Galatians 5:22..

**6:7 By the word of truth, by the power of God.** In other words, "We came to you preaching the true doctrine, not like the false teachers— the Judaizers—who are adulterating the word of God. I delivered to you the doctrine that we received from God, because it is my responsibility as a servant of God to teach you the truth, and the truth will set you free. I did not come to you trusting in my own powers, my abilities, talents, nor gifts, but I relied completely on God. I did not come with the excellence of speech or the wisdom of humans, but I came to you with the power of God and the power of the Holy Spirit."

**by the armor of righteousness on the right hand and on the left.** St. Paul was trying to tell them here that in order to be righteous, I came to you as a righteous person, but in order to be righteous, you have to put on the whole armor of God." And you can read about the armor of God in Ephesians 6:11–18. You cannot live a righteous life without putting on the armor of God. There are offensive weapons and defensive weapons; you carry the shield with your left hand, while the sword is carried with your right hand. The sword is the word of God and the shield is the shield of faith. By the shield of faith,

I was able to protect my heart, and by the word of God—the sword in my right hand—I was able to defeat the devil and live a righteous life, that is why he said, "on the right hand and on the left hand." We have the armor to protect us on all sides, everywhere and in all occasions—that is how we will live a righteous life. Perhaps we will sit on the right hand and on the left; the right hand signifies prosperity, the left hand signifies adversity. He was saying, "We have the armor of God to help and protect us, both in prosperity and in adversity. We have the word of truth, the power of God, the shield of faith to defend us in prosperity and in adversity." In these verses, St. Paul was able to explain to them how he did not give offense, how he kept the service and the ministry from being blamed— by his patience, by his endurance, and also by bearing the fruit of the Spirit, and thus showing God's grace in his life. What about the conflicting reports and conflicting reactions about him? He said, "Also with these conflicting reports, I showed no offence."

Many times, as priests, we receive honor that is not ours; it is the honor of the priesthood of Christ. At times God allows for us to receive this honor and at other times dishonor; we should receive the dishonor without being angry or frustrated, rather we should follow the example of St. Paul as servants of Christ, as His ambassadors.

**by evil report and good report.** Many times people praise us, but other times people falsely accuse us, and as we accept the good report, so we need to also accept the evil report. This should not change my heart, this should not make me frustrated or angry.

**as deceivers.** Sometimes people say about us that we are false teachers and teach false doctrine; they said so about St. Paul.

**and yet true.** Maybe in the perceptions of some people we are deceivers, but before God we are true. This truth is demonstrated by the nature of the doctrine that we are teaching, as well as by our righteous and holy lives

**6:8     by honor and dishonor.** "Sometimes people respected us as ministers of God, other times people despised us. Whether we are honored or dishonored, this does not change anything in our ministry. We did not lose our patience, we did not lose our righteousness, we did not get angry with the people who despised us."

**6:9     as unknown, and yet well known.** In this indifferent world, maybe we are unknown, maybe we are not famous like the movie actors or of the sports stars and trainers; maybe the people of God and servants of God are not known like a lot of these figures of the world, but we are well-known to God. God knows how much His servants labor for Him, how many sacrifices they offer every day. God is actually counting our steps. God told us that "Even a cup of water given to one of My brethren will not be forgotten." Maybe the world does not know us, and yet we are well-known before God.

**as dying, and behold we live.** We are always exposed to death. We receive death threats, and we endure persecution and suffering for the name of Christ, yet we are preserved. Even if they kill us, like John the Baptist, we have eternal life. That is why "as dying," we die every day in Christ, yet we are alive in Him. Maybe they can touch the body, but they cannot touch the soul within.

**as chastened, and yet not killed.** God our Father, for our purity and righteousness, may allow us to be chastened. As a father disciplines and chastens his son so too are we chastened by God, as we read in Psalm 118, "With chastening He chastened me, but He did not deliver me to death." Many times we are chastened yet not killed, because God spares our lives. He chastens us to make us better and to improve us. Not to kill us nor to destroy us.

**6:10** **as sorrowful, yet always rejoicing.** Yes, during this suffering, when we face all these tribulations, we might grieve. When we see people drifting away from Christ, when we see

people not repenting, it might make our heart grieve. Yet we rejoice in hope, in confidence that God will deliver us and will deliver His people, because it is the good pleasure of God to give us the Kingdom. "At the same time that we are sorrowful, this sorrow is full of joy. You will weep and lament, but I will see you and your sorrow will turn into joy—as sorrowful, yet always rejoicing."

**as poor.** "Poor" because we do not have the wealth of the world, the riches of the world, but we make many men rich by offering them the riches of Christ, of the Kingdom of God, the riches that do not corrupt and cannot be stolen. We offer people the true riches of Christ..

**as having nothing, and yet possessing all things.** We truly give up everything for Christ. We do not own anything from the possessions of this world. "And yet possessing all things," because we have Christ, and if we have Christ, we have all things.

**6:11** **"O Corinthians! We have spoken openly to you, our heart is wide open.** In the previous verses, St. Paul showed them how his ministry was approved, how in spite of all these hardships he presented himself as a servant of Christ with no offense nor blemish to the ministry, but rather accepted all the suffering in order to make his ministry approved by God. Now, in verse 11 he tells them, "We have done all these things because we love you and we care about your salvation. We want you to return to God. But the more we love you, the less you love us." ❖ "I speak to you with the utmost of freedom because of my affection for you, because of my love for you. Our hearts expanded to take you in, and to take all your interest in and keep you in. Our hearts are expanded by the Holy Spirit; because the fruit of the Spirit is love, the Holy Spirit widened my heart—expanded it in order to include you in our hearts." ❖ "We did not hide anything of the mysteries of God; our hearts are wide open to you, but you rejected us. There are no barriers in our hearts. You can come and speak into our hearts. It is not we who restrict you (as noted in the next verse], but you are restricted by your own affections. You do not have a narrow place in our affection, but unfortunately, we do not have the same place in your hearts— we do not have the same place in your affection."

**6:12 You are not restricted by us, but you are restricted by your own affections.** In some translations of the Bible it says, "You are restricted by your own bowels." The word "bowels" is used in Scripture to denote the most tender affection. He was telling them, "Our hearts are full of love and tenderness toward you, but we do not have the same place in your hearts." "So now, as my children, I command you—

and I have the right to command you, as your father—I want you to repay me with love. As we love you, I expect you to love us."

**6:13 Now in return for the same (I speak as to children), you also be open.** Love for love. I am speaking with authority as your father because you are my children, you also be open. Open your hearts to us, open your hearts and give us place in your hearts. Repay me for my affection toward you. I speak to you as to my children whom I have a right to command to love me, as I love you." "When I speak to you to be open, you need to be wise and have discernment." "Be open" does not mean to be under the same yoke with the unbelievers.

**6:14 Do not be unequally yoked together with unbelievers.** St. Paul was mentally recalling Deuteronomy 22:10 and Leviticus 19:19—that believers should not pair off with unbelievers; St. Paul was making a wonderful argument here. This verse is mainly about intermarriage. That is why in Christianity we cannot marry a Christian to a non-Christian. This is one of the major differences between the Catholics and the Orthodox: the Catholic Church allows marriage between Catholic and non-Christian, while the Orthodox do not. We ask them this question: when you marry a Catholic to a non-Christian, is it a sacramental marriage? Does the Holy Spirit descend and unite these two persons? As St. Paul said, "There is no fellowship," that is why we do not intermarry; believers should marry believers. Although St. Paul had intermarriage in mind, he was also speaking about association between believers in non-believer festivals. Any close fellowship with a nonbeliever is prohibited.

**For what fellowship has righteousness with lawlessness?** He told them not to be unequally yoked (the yoke is a piece of wood between two animals); do not be under the same yoke, as in marriage, with the unbeliever. Why? "For what fellowship has righteousness with lawlessness?" We follow the Law of God, and by following the Law of God we live righteous lives, but the unbelievers are without law (they do not follow the Law of Christ—which is why he described them as "lawlessness").

How will you follow the Law of God, and then marry someone who is not following the Law of God? There is no fellowship between the believer and lawlessness. How then would a believer keep up the confession of Christianity, being associated with the unrighteous—those who do not follow the Law of God?

**And what communion has light with darkness?** As the Lord told us, "You are the light of the world." How are we the light of the world? Because in us we have Christ, the Son of righteousness. Can you put light and darkness together? Those who do not have Christ are darkness. Even we (before Christ, as we say in Isaiah and in the Divine Liturgy), "were living in darkness and in the shadow of death, but when the Morningstar, (when Jesus) shone in our hearts, we became light." So, is there communion between light and darkness? Absolutely not, that is why the believer cannot marry an unbeliever.

**6:15 And what accord has Christ with Belial?** Belial is a heathen god, an idol like Beelzebub. This is put as a reference to Satan. Christ has nothing in common with Satan; there is no accord between Christ and Satan, so how can a believer who is following Christ have close intimacy with a person who is still under the dominion of Satan? All the nonbelievers are under the dominion of Satan; they have not moved from the kingdom of Satan to the Kingdom of the Son of God, so how can you have a close, intimate relationship with those who are under the dominion of Satan?.

**Or what part has a believer with an unbeliever?** The question posed here highlights a notion that does not make sense. If you believe in Christ, how will you be in oneness—because in marriage "the two shall become one"—with a nonbeliever?

**6:16** **And what agreement has the temple of God with idols?** St. Paul was saying, "As the temple of God has nothing to do with the temple of the idols, in the same way, we Christians (the saints, the temple of God) should be separated completely from unbelievers. There is no communion between the temple of God and the temple of idols. Those who eat from the temples of idols, those who follow other religions, cannot be in communion with the children of God. What agreement has the temple of God with idols?

**For you are the temple of the living God.** You Christians, believers, who were baptized and Chrismated and received the Holy Spirit, you are the temple of the Living God. You are the temple of the Living God. As the Holy Spirit lives in the church and sanctifies the church, in the same way, the Holy Spirit lives in you and you are the temple of Christ. You are a church, a consecrated place for Christ, you are the sanctuary of Christ.

**As God has said: "I will dwell in them and walk among them."** He was saying here, "You are the temple of the Living God, as God has said, "I will dwell in them, I have My dwelling." He tabernacled among us, He dwelt in us. The Holy Spirit dwells in you, God

dwells in His people. As we read in Leviticus 26:12 and in Exodus 25:2, "I will dwell in them, I will walk among them," Emmanuel—God is with us.

**"I will be their God, and they shall be My people."** Here it is clear that God is dwelling in us, with us, among us. There is no fellowship, no communion between the believer and the unbeliever. God is our Father, but unbelievers cannot call God their Father, so how can we—the children of God—be in communion, in oneness, in unity with unbelievers? He is our God and we are His people, but the unbeliever is under the domain of Satan.

**6:17** **Therefore "Come out from among them and be separate, says the Lord. Do not touch what is unclean, and I will receive you."** it is a call to cleanse one's soul from paganism, as we read in Isaiah 52:11. Come out from among them, do not dwell among them, "be separate, says the Lord. Do not touch what is unclean." Our cleanness is from Christ, from the Holy Spirit who purifies us, who sanctifies us, but if we have fellowship with the nonbeliever, we are touching the unclean. The commandment here is: "Be separate ... do not touch what is unclean, and I will receive you," which means that if you touch what is unclean, if you marry outside your faith, this means God will not receive you, you will not receive the blessings of Christ, you will not receive the promises of Christ. But if you separate yourself and do not touch what is unclean, then "I will receive you; I will receive you and I will give you My blessings and My promises." Here St. Paul was actually quoting several verses from Jeremiah 31:1 and 9, from Isaiah 43:6, from Joshua 1:27. It is as if St. Paul was telling us, "It is the will of God that His children, the worshippers, the believers, should be separate from the world. Yes, we live in the world, but we are separate from the world. As the sunlight shines in the world but is separate from the world, so we, the children of God, shine in the world but we are separate from the world.

**6:18** "I will be a Father to you, and you shall be My sons and daughters, says the Lord Almighty." If you come out from among them, become separate, do not touch what is unclean, then "I will receive you. I will be a Father to you and you shall be My sons and daughters. You will be My children and I will give you the honor of sonship, says the Lord Almighty." Then He will receive and accept us as His own children. Which means, if a person marries or associates with the unbeliever, he is rejecting his sonship; he cannot be a son anymore. Many times people come and argue, "Why can't you give us communion? Why does the church reject us when we marry outside our church?" Actually,

the question here is: who rejected who? Did the church reject you, or are you, by marrying outside the church, the one who rejected the church? You are rejecting the church, you are rejecting your sonship, that is why you cannot have communion. If you have communion with unbelievers then you cannot have communion with Christ at the same time. There is no communion between light and darkness, between Christ and Belial, between the temple of God and the temple of idols.

## Chapter 6 Questions

1. How does St. Paul describe himself as he pleads with the Corinthians to? (v.1)

2. Why was St. Paul so careful not to give offense in anything? (v.3)

3. List some of the physical sufferings which commended St. Paul as a Minister of God. (v.4-5)

4. List those areas where St. Paul demonstrated his integrity as a minister of God. (v.6-7)

5. List the contrasting experiences St. Paul had as a minister of God. (v.9-10)

6. How does St. Paul describe his affection toward the Corinthians? (v.11)

7. What does he say about the Corinthians' affections toward him?

8. What charge does St. Paul give concerning our relation to those in the world? (v.14)

9. List the contrasting pairs that St. Paul uses to show the strangeness of believers being unequally yoked with unbelievers. (v.14-16)

10. What is necessary to receive the promise of having God as our Father who dwells among us? (v.17-18)

# 7

## Chapter Outline

**7:1 Therefore, having these promises, beloved.** What are these promises? The promises that he mentioned to them in Chapter 6, verses 17 and 18. God promised them that if they live away from the ungodly people, do not mingle with the ungodly people, do not marry nonbelievers, then He will accept them to Him, and He will be their Father and they will be His children. Moreover, the Holy Spirit will dwell in them and they will become the temple of the Holy Spirit.

**let us cleanse ourselves from all filthiness of the flesh and spirit.** St. Paul was differentiating between the sins of the flesh and the sins of the spirit. There are sins related to the flesh, and sins related to the spirit. He is asking them to live in spiritual maturity. What are the sins of the flesh? All the sensual sins like addiction or sexual immorality are sins related to the flesh. Our spirit can also be defiled by another list of sins, like the list that St. Paul mentions in Galatians 5:19 & 21 such as anger, bitterness, wrath, envy, and hatred.

St. Paul was saying, "Now, having all these promises from God, let us cleanse ourselves from the sins of the flesh and also from the sins of the spirit."

**perfecting holiness in the fear of God.** what does it mean to "perfect holiness?" There are two commandments: be perfect as your Father in heaven is perfect and be holy as your Father in heaven is holy. Therefore, we as Christians should strive for perfect holiness. Yes, nobody can claim that "I became perfect in holiness," but we should grow and perfect our holiness. We should continually strive for greater holiness. How can we achieve this? How can we perfect our holiness? How can we grow in our holiness which St. Paul mentioned in his letter to the Hebrews (12:14): "Without holiness nobody can see God?" Holiness is a condition to see God. As it is written in Matthew 5:8, "Blessed are the pure in heart for they shall see God." The only way to perfect your holiness is to walk in the fear of God and keep the fear of God before your eyes. That is why he said, "Perfecting holiness in the fear of God." Ask yourself, what makes a person commit any sin? The fear of God does not exist in his heart. Unfortunately, many times we fear men but we do not fear God. If someone is watching me, maybe I will be embarrassed to commit sin, but if I am by myself (which is not true because even if I am alone God is watching me) I do not fear God and allow myself to commit many sins.

St. John Climacus wrote in his book The Ladder of Divine Ascent, "Many people fear animals more than they fear God," even giving an example: If a thief goes to rob a house and a dog starts to bark, maybe the thief will run. Thus, he feared the dog although he did not fear God. That is why if you want to perfect holiness you need to walk in the fear of God.

**7:2    Open your hearts to us.** In Chapter 6 (verse 11) he told them, "Our hearts (the hearts of St. Paul and the Apostles) are wide open to you, so you are not restricted in our hearts, you have a place in our hearts. But you are restricted in your hearts, and we do not have a place in them. We love you but you do not love us." That was why he told them, "Open your hearts to us, why are you angry with us? Open your hearts to us. Why do you not love us? Make room in your hearts for us and for our admonition."

**we have wronged no one.** Even the offender, the one whom I excommunicated—I did not wrong him. He received his just consequence. He lived in sexual immorality and to excommunicate him, I actually did that to lead him to repentance. So, we have wronged no man, even in the severe charges of the first Letter, like this offender.".

**we have corrupted no one, we have cheated no one.** Some of the opponents of St. Paul were claiming that his teaching corrupted the people, because he asked them not to follow the Law since we are now living by the grace of God. That was why St. Paul told them, "We have wronged no one, we have corrupted no one, we have cheated no one." Other accusations made against St. Paul were that he was asking the people to follow him, not to follow God, and that he was "cheating them" (as if he was demanding financial support) because in 1 Corinthians 9 he spoke about how the church should support the servants of the church.

**7:3  I do not say this to condemn; for I have said before that you are in our hearts, to die together and to live together.** St. Paul was saying, "When I am telling you that we have wronged no one, we have corrupted no one, we have cheated no one, I am not accusing you of making these charges against me. I know very well that it is only my adversaries who say these accusations against me; I am not condemning you." "I want to assure you as I said before" (in Chapter 6:11–12), he had told them, "Our hearts are widely open to you and you live in our heart." He was telling them, "If you live in my heart, then if we die, we will die together, and if we live, we live together; you are part of me. I am not condemning you because if I condemn you, I am condemning myself. You are a part of me." ✤ "I said before that you are in our hearts, to die together and to live together." This is actually a very, very beautiful description of how the relationship should be between the pastor and the flock. It should be a relationship of unity and oneness, to live in our hearts so that we will rejoice together and suffer together, we will live together and die together because all of us are one, and we are one in the body of Christ. In the Old Testament, the high priest would wear a breastplate that had twelve stones. These twelve stones had the names of the twelve tribes, as if he was carrying his people in his heart. The priest should carry the people in his heart as St. Paul said, "You are in our hearts and so, we will live together and we will die together. This is the best expression of St. Paul's undying affection towards them.

**great is my boasting on your behalf.** When the priest or pastor sees his flock living a life of repentance, he will boast and be proud of them—he will be boasting on their behalf.

**I am filled with comfort. I am exceedingly joyful in all our tribulation.** "Yes, every day we face hardship, tribulation, and affliction, but when we hear good news about you and your life with Christ, this comforts us, this makes us exceedingly joyful, even in the midst of our tribulation." ✤ Believe me, what saddens or makes the heart of a priest sad and sorrowful, is when he sees his people and his children drifting away from Christ. But when he sees his children growing in the love of Christ, then, even in the midst of the most difficult hardship or tribulation, he becomes joyful and comforted by the repentance of his people.

**7:4    Great is my boldness of speech toward you.** Now St. Paul is starting to tell them about how the news that he received from Titus filled his heart with joy, so he uses four different expressions. The first expression is: "Great is my boldness of speech toward you," as if he is saying, "When I speak about you, I speak with confidence, I speak with boldness because I know that you had repented, I know that you are obedient to the Gospel of Christ. So, when I speak about you, I speak with boldness, I speak with confidence."

**7:5    For indeed, when we came to Macedonia, our bodies had no rest, but we were troubled on every side. Outside were conflicts, inside were fears."** When St. Paul came from Ephesus to Troas, he expected to meet Titus there with word from Corinth concerning the effect of his first Letter, but he did not find Titus in Troas. That was why he said in 2 Corinthians 2:12, "I did not have rest in my soul," and that is what he speaks about in this verse. Not finding Titus in Troas, he went to Macedonia; he was so distressed in mind, in spirit, and also in flesh. His flesh had no rest; he was so tired. Most times, when a person is psychologically stressed or stressed out, his body will also be tired. That was why he told them, "When we came from Macedonia to Troas, we were so tired physically, our bodies had no rest and we were troubled from every side. From outside there were conflicts— conflicts with the enemies of Christ, conflicts with the opponents, conflicts with the Judaizers who want to bring you back to the Jewish law (to be saved by the Jewish law). From outside there were conflicts and from inside we had fears lest the church suffer loss, lest this man who was excommunicated never returns, lest there be a division in the church due to the first Letter." Can you imagine with me the condition of St. Paul? From inside he has fears, worries about the church in Corinth, about every soul in this church, and from outside, conflict with the enemies of Christ. On top of this, physically he was so tired. That was his condition when he came from Troas to Macedonia, especially because he did not meet Titus in Troas.

**7:6    Nevertheless God, who comforts the downcast.** I like how St. Paul described God here, "God, who comforts the downcast." If you feel down, if you feel that you are desperate, that there is no hope, or that all the doors are closed in front of you, remember

that God is the hope of the hopeless; God is the help for the helpless.

Think about the many examples in the Scriptures—and also in our lives—like Mary and Martha who lost hope in their brother, but God was the hope for the hopeless and was able to raise Lazarus from the dead. St. Paul knew very well that God would not leave him in such a condition, after he had suffered from outside and from inside.

**comforted us by the coming of Titus.** He says this because Titus brought him joyful news of the repentance and reformation of the church of Corinth. This news turned his suffering, his affliction, into joy. So, all of a sudden, after he was very troubled and oppressed from outside and from within, now he was comforted and all this affliction turned to joy.

**7:7    And not only by his coming, but also by the consolation with which he was comforted in you, when he told us of your earnest desire, your mourning, your zeal for me, so that I rejoiced even more.** "The first reason for my joy is because I saw Titus—my beloved disciple, my beloved son, my beloved fellow worker. I was so happy to see him," so he rejoiced at meeting a beloved fellow laborer like Titus. The second reason is that Titus himself was comforted by the repentance of the Corinthians, so he was rejoiced because Titus was comforted by the repentance and the reformation of the Corinthians. The third reason is that when he heard the news about the church in Corinth, he was comforted. What news? He mentioned three things. (1) Number one, he heard about their earnest desire to cleanse themselves from all the filthiness of the flesh and spirit. He became so happy. (2) Another reason was their mourning; they became sorrowful, as St. Paul will explain, with godly sorrow. They mourned over the reproof of their sins, they grieved because they disappointed God by having such sin in their lives. (3) And number three, their zeal for him, as he told them, "Your zeal for me." Even when he had written them such a harsh letter, they did not take a stand against St. Paul, but became more zealous and more affectionate; they had zeal to please St. Paul because they knew St. Paul cared about them. As a father, he wanted to shepherd them to the green pastures, beside the still waters. That is why they trusted St. Paul; they were not angry with him when they read his letter. "So that I rejoiced even more"— he rejoiced because he saw Titus was joyful, because he heard about their earnest desire, their mourning, and their zeal for him.

**7:8  For even if I made you sorry with my letter, I do not regret it; though I did regret it. For I perceive that the same epistle made you sorry, though only for a while.** St.

Paul told them, "After I wrote the letter to you, I realized that it would make you sorry, and at one point I regretted sending this letter to you. But when Titus came and told me that, 'This letter changed their lives, led them to repentance, reformed the church there,' I did not regret that I had sent the letter." "I regretted because I feared it would not produce the desired fruit, I feared that I may lose you or I may lose some of you, and as a father I cannot afford losing any of you. But now, after I heard the news from Titus, I no longer regret sending this letter, especially that this sorrow was temporary. Yes, my letter—my epistle—made you sorrow, though only for a while, but now with repentance your sorrow turned into what? Into joy. So, this sorrow was not permanent; it was only temporary."

**7:9  Now I rejoice, not that you were made sorry, but that your sorrow led to repentance.** I am not happy because I made you sorry, but that your sorrow led to repentance. St. Paul was saying, "Now I rejoice, not because I made you sorry—a father would never rejoice when he makes his son sorrowful—but I rejoice because your sorrow led to repentance."  ❖ Here, I want to differentiate between sorrow and repentance. St. Paul said that sorrow led to repentance, so sorrow is different from repentance. Many people, when they experience remorse over sin think that they have repented, but no. Many people may actually develop remorse without repentance.

**For you were made sorry in a godly manner.** There is a godly sorrow and there is a sorrow of the world. The godly sorrow leads to repentance, but the ungodly sorrow or the sorrow of the world, leads to death. What a big difference! He told them, "You were made sorry in a godly manner." Godly sorrow is sorrowing in a way that is pleasing to God and it is the very work of the Holy Spirit in our hearts. When the Holy Spirit convicts me, I will develop godly sorrow.

**that you might suffer loss from us in nothing.** What added to his pleasure is that his writing to them produced an effect. The letter had not been in the least harmful to anyone, did not hurt anyone, did not make anyone stray from the church or stay away from the church. This sorrow was developed in them in such a way that not only were they not hurt in their souls, but they actually repented and bore the fruit of repentance. Their church did not suffer any loss, even the offender repented and returned. Here, as a true shepherd, he cares about every single person. That is why he said, "That you might suffer loss from us in nothing" - you will not lose anything, our letter should not harm you, our letter did not harm you, our letter did not hurt you. No one was offended by the letter, no one was lost by the letter. ✷ This should be the focus of the clergy in their service—

not to lose any one. Even when we use discipline, we have to know that the purpose of discipline is bringing people to the church, not pushing people away from the church. If with my discipline I am actually pushing people away from the church, this is wrong; it has produced the opposite result. That is why St. Paul was comforted when he realized that his letter did not offend, hurt, or harm anyone. Even the offender himself, the person who committed adultery with his father's wife, which was actually the occasion for all this trouble, was recovered and restored by his epistle.

**7:10  For godly sorrow produces repentance leading to salvation, not to be regretted.** St. Paul differentiates between the godly sorrow and the sorrow of the world. He said there are certain steps here: the Holy Spirit will convict you when you commit a sin, then when the Holy Spirit convicts you, you need to develop this sorrow. Then with this sorrow the second step is to repent. Repentance is the changing of the mind and the behavior; renewal of your mind so that there will be fruit—instead of being a robber you will be honest, instead of being a liar you will be faithful, instead of being involved with sexual immorality you will be pure. Sorrow is when we develop this remorse within our hearts, but repentance is the change in the mind and in the behavior. A real change will happen in the person that everyone will see and notice. Repentance is the result of godly sorrow. With your repentance you are securing your salvation, because the Lord said, "Unless you repent you will all perish," (Luke 13:3 & 5). There is no salvation without repentance, and the effect of this repentance is never regretted. We never heard that St. Moses the Black or St. Augustine or St. Pelagia (all these penitent saints) ever regretted their return to God.

**but the sorrow of the world produces death.** Let me give you an example about the sorrow of the world, to differentiate it from the godly sorrow. The best example is that of Judas. After Judas betrayed the Lord Jesus Christ, he was sorrowful and said, "I regret that I delivered innocent blood to you," but this sorrow of Judas was initiated by his ego, not by the Holy Spirit. What does this mean? Many times when we commit a sin we say, "How can I who am a servant of the church, who am a deacon, who am an active church member, who am a believer for so long, how did I fall into such a sin?" This sorrow and grief is not because I disappointed God, it is not because I disobeyed God, but it is because of "How could I commit such a sin? How could I be embarrassed in front of the community? How could people think about me in such a negative way?" This sorrow is initiated by the ego, but the sorrow that is initiated by the Holy Spirit (and is the reason behind my sorrow and grief) is because I grieved and saddened

the heart of God, I disobeyed God, I made God sorrowful because of my sin.

⛨  Another very important difference between godly sorry and the sorrow of this world, is that the godly sorrow is full of hope because it is initiated by the Holy Spirit, while the sorrow of the world is full of fear; there is no hope in this sorrow. The best example of godly sorrow is the sorrow of St. Peter after he denied the Lord Jesus Christ three times. He wept bitterly but he did not kill himself, because he had confidence that Christ would forgive and accept him. The sorrow of the world results in despair and leads to destruction of life and eternal death. People regret the sorrow of the world, but no one regrets godly sorrow, because godly sorrow leads to repentance, leads to salvation, and is not to be regretted. The sorrow of the world leads to destruction, despair, hopelessness, which will be regretted.

**7:11**   **For observe this very thing, that you sorrowed in a godly manner.** Now St. Paul will give them the evidence, the proof, that their sorrow was a godly sorrow, because it led to repentance and actually produced the fruit of repentance in them. He mentions here seven fruits; this sorrow led to repentance and actually bore seven fruits of repentance!

**What diligence it produced in you.** (1) of 7 *fruits of repentance*. The people in Corinth were indifferent to sin (they did not take any action when they heard about this man who committed adultery with his father's wife) but after St. Paul sent them the letter, they were no longer indifferent, they were sensitive to sins and diligent in keeping the purity of the church.

**what clearing of yourselves.** (2) of 7 *fruits of repentance.* Now that they had acknowledged their indifference, their neglect, their sins, now they wanted to clear themselves from this sin. They showed diligence in purifying themselves of this sin—they prayed, they declared that they did not approve of this sin, and they took a stand in participating in the excommunication of this person by not eating with him, by not drinking with him, by not associating with him. They took a stand and thus cleared themselves and proved they did not approve or validate his action.

**what indignation.** (3) of 7 *fruits of repentance.* The third fruit is indignation. Indignation is holy anger. Not every anger is a bad anger; there is a type of anger that is holy anger. It is "holy" anger when it is directed toward sin. The Bible usually uses the word indignation when it speaks about holy anger. Everyone in Corinth became indignant against the sin that had disgraced the church and had taken the grace of the church away. They became angry at sin, and if you get angry at sin you will never fall in sin again.

**what fear.** (4) of 7 *fruits of repentance.* This sorrow produced in them the fear of God. Do you remember in verse 1 he told them, "Perfecting holiness in the fear of God?" and as I said, if a person walks in the fear of God, he will never disobey God. So they developed the fear of God as well as the fear of grieving the apostles and the ministers of God. They also feared lest the sin and corruption spread in the church, because sin is contagious.

**what vehement desire.** (5) of 7 *fruits of repentance.* The desire to see the apostle, comfort him, desire to be kept away from evil, desire to honor and please God in their lives.

**what zeal.** (6) of 7 *fruits of repentance.* Zeal for God and for His glory, zeal to keep the church pure and clean, zeal in requiring the discipline of the church as the discipline of the church is needed to keep the church pure. Like when the Lord Jesus Christ on Hosanna Sunday came outside the temple, the Disciples remembered this verse: "The zeal of Your house has eaten me up." So why did the Lord purify the Temple? Because of zeal. Zeal will lead a person to discipline, in order to purify and cleanse the Church of God.

**what vindication! In all things you proved yourselves to be clear in this matter.** (7) of 7 *fruits of repentance.* Vindication—vindication means to punish the sin; punish all disobedience and punish the offender with a purpose to bring him back to Christ. This is very important; the purpose of punishment is not condemnation, but restoration. The Lord said, "I did not come to condemn the world but I came to save the world." When we punish or when we discipline, the purpose of punishment is not condemnation; the purpose of punishment is restoration. He told them, "Do you want evidence that you sorrowed in a godly manner? See what diligence it produced in you, what clearing of yourselves it produced in you, what indignation it produced in you, what fear it produced in you, what vehement desire it produced in you, what zeal it produced in you, what vindication? In all things, you proved yourselves to be cleared in this manner." Actually this verse is very amazing to me. They were indifferent to the sin, they were negligent in taking action, and St. Paul rebuked them harshly in the first Letter because they did not take action. But now St. Paul was telling them, "In all things you proved yourselves to be cleared in this matter," and this shows to me the forgiving spirit of St. Paul.

Once the people in Corinth repented, acknowledged their sins, St. Paul told them, "You are completely cleared in this matter." Yes, it is as we read, how great repentance is, because repentance can change adulterers into virgins. St. Paul was telling them, "It is now clear to me that you did not consent to this sin, you did not approve of this sin." Although at first they were unconcerned about the sin, but by discovering their true repentance for their negligence, St.

Paul perceived them as if they had not offended at all, as if they were clear.

**7:12 Therefore, although I wrote to you, I did not do it for the sake of him who had done the wrong, nor for the sake of him who suffered wrong, but that our care for you in the sight of God might appear to you.** I did not write my first Letter only for the sake of the offender to bring him to repentance, I did not write it only for the sake of the person who was offended or hurt by this offense" — which is the offender's father and his wife, unless his wife participated in the sin by her own will, by her own desire — but St. Paul was saying, "I did not write my harsh letter to you because of the offender or those offended, although that was part of my intention, but the main purpose was to show you my care for the whole church." As he said in the first letter, a small lump will leaven the whole church. If we leave this sin in the church it will grow and spread among the whole church. "So I actually took this action to keep your church holy and pure and thus you will know that I care for you, that our care for you in the sight of God might appear to you, so that you know how much we love you, how much we care about you, how much we want your church to be holy and to be pure." Then in the last four verses of the chapter he talks about how Titus was joyful, and how the joy of Titus was also reflected on St. Paul.

**7:13    Therefore we have been comforted in your comfort. And we rejoiced exceedingly more for the joy of Titus, because his spirit has been refreshed by you all.** St. Paul told them, "When we went to Macedonia we were troubled, but once we heard of your news, we were comforted by your comfort; you are the reason for my comfort." He is expressing his joy over the change in the church of Corinth, a joy which also refreshed the heart of Titus. "Your news made me joyous, your news also refreshed the heart of Titus. And because Titus was joyful, we also became joyful."

**7:14    For if in anything I have boasted to him about you, I am not ashamed. But as we spoke all things to you in truth, even so our boasting to Titus was found true.** Paul sent Titus to Corinth telling him, "You know what, the people in Corinth are very good people. Yes, this sin happened but I am sure that now you will find all of them repenting." Perhaps he said this to encourage Titus to go there, to support him. Then when Titus went there and found the people repenting, St. Paul was telling them, "You did not embarrass me, I am not ashamed of having told Titus that you are good and you had received my letter in the right way." That is why he said, "For if in anything I have boasted to him, to Titus, about you, I am not ashamed—I am not ashamed that what

I told him was not true but, as I always say the truth, as we spoke all things to you in truth, even so our boasting about you to Titus was found true. Titus found you to be repentant people as I had told him. If I have boasted anything about you to Titus, your prompt repentance showed that my boasting was true, as we speak all things also in truth."

**7:15    And his affections are greater for you as he remembers the obedience of you all, how with fear and trembling you received him.** "Even Titus's love toward you is now greater, why? Because every time he remembers your obedience, your repentance (because they repented as a sign of their obedience to St. Paul and to Titus) and how in fear and trembling you repented and returned to God, this makes Titus love you more and more." Titus was not received with disobedience in the church of Corinth, but in a humble and repentant Christian spirit, which actually increased his affection toward them greatly. Also, this obedience and this repentance with fear and trembling increased the confidence of St. Paul toward them.

**7:16    Therefore I rejoice that I have confidence in you in everything.** In other words, "Now I am confident. You proved to me that you are trustworthy; that when I sent you the letter, you responded in the right way. I am greatly confident concerning you and because of this confidence, I rejoice greatly because of you."

## Chapter 7 Questions

1. In view of the promises in the preceding chapter, what two things does St. Paul admonish us to do?

2. What plea does St. Paul repeat that was made in chapter 6?

3. What was St. Paul's condition when he first came to Macedonia?

4. How did God comfort him in Macedonia?

5. What about the Corinthians' sorrow led St. Paul to rejoice?

6. What is the difference between "godly sorrow" and "sorrow of the world"?

7. Why had St. Paul written to the Corinthians?

**8:1 Moreover, brethren, we make known to you the grace of God bestowed on the churches of Macedonia.** It is clear that the mother church in Jerusalem was in need, and the churches all over the world supported the mother church in Jerusalem. Two things happened in Jerusalem. Number one, famine struck the land and number two, some trouble in the state led to the Jewish war and resulted in a state of destitution and poverty. That was why all the churches felt the responsibility to support the mother church in Jerusalem. The fact that they were at a distance from Jerusalem did not diminish the claims of the suffering brethren for help. They did not say, "We do not care." Rather, they actually collected money and sent messengers to the mother church. Although they were living in Corinth in Greece (Macedonia in Asia Minor, current day Turkey), they felt responsible to support the church in Jerusalem. What are the churches of Macedonia that he is speaking about in this verse? All the Grecian countries north of Achaia. These were the churches of Macedonia, like Philippi, like Galatia. St. Paul was telling them, when these churches, when the congregations of these churches were filled by the grace of God, they actually became exceedingly generous and gave with abundance to help the church in Jerusalem. The more you are filled with the grace of God, the more this will appear in your generosity and in your mercy to others.

**8:2 that in a great trial of affliction.** St. Paul was telling them, "I want you to know that the churches in Macedonia were in a great trial of affliction. The words 'trial of affliction' imply persecution—perhaps the Jewish persecution against the Christians. But although they went through this great trial of affliction, they did not use it as an excuse for not giving." Many times when we undergo a bad economy or some hardship, we take it as an excuse not to give. St. Paul is telling us here that the churches in Macedonia, although they were in a great trial of affliction, they gave abundantly.

**the abundance of their joy and their deep poverty abounded.** St. Paul was explaining to us how the grace of God was working in them when he used two contradictory terms: "The abundance of their joy and their deep poverty." When we think about deep poverty, we think they should be sad, but what St. Paul is saying is that the greater their poverty, the greater was the abundance of their joy. Because the more a person is in need, the more he will rely on God, and when you rely on God more, God will comfort you and that is why you will experience great joy.

**in the riches of their liberality.** Although they were in a great trial of affliction and although they were deeply poor, yet because of the grace of God in their lives they were also abundant in their joy; they had excessive joy. This joy helped them in giving with liberality and abundance. The poverty and the joy had the effect not of producing stinginess with gifts, but in abounding in liberality.

**8:3    For I bear witness that according to their ability, yes, and beyond their ability.** They not only gave up to their ability, but above and beyond their ability—that is why their generosity and liberality were so rich. Take the example of the widow who gave all that she had - the two mites ; or the example of the widow at Sidon, when Elijah went to her and she had a small amount of oil and a little flour and she told him, "There is a famine, and I will make a cake for me and my son and we will eat it and die." But Elijah told her, "Make one for me first," and she put him ahead of herself and her son. Because she put him first and gave abundantly in spite of her poverty, in spite of the great famine that they were

facing at that time, when she gave with liberality, God actually blessed the oil and flour in her house until the end of the famine.

**they were freely willing.** St. Paul said a very important word, "They were freely willing"; they were willing of themselves, not with urging. No one urged them or pushed them or forced them or made them guilty in order to give, but they were freely willing to give. This is actually the work of the grace of God in our hearts.

**8:4    imploring us with much urgency that we would receive the gift.** Perhaps St. Paul had told them, "You are in poverty, you are facing a great trial, so keep your money for yourselves," but they had actually refused, which is why he said, "Imploring us with much urgency." They insisted on doing more than the apostle felt that they ought to do, and they insisted on giving above and beyond. It was as if they were saying to St. Paul, "Why do you want to deprive us of this blessing? This is the fellowship of serving the saints." God said, "Whatever you do unto these little children, you do it unto Me. I was hungry and you gave Me food, I was thirsty and you gave Me drink. So, it is as if they were saying to St. Paul, "Why do you want to deprive us of this blessing?"

and the fellowship of the ministering to the saints. This is why they implored him with much urgency, that they would receive the gift of the fellowship—that is how they understood the gift—"The fellowship of the ministering to the saints." When they give, it is as if they are in fellowship with the poor, the saints, and they are getting the blessing of serving and ministering to the saints.

**8:5** And not only as we had hoped, but they first gave themselves to the Lord. This is the key to their joy, the key to their abundance in giving— that they first gave themselves to the Lord. When you give yourself to God, you are actually giving all that you have, all that you possess, and all that you own to God. You feel that you own nothing; everything belongs to God.

and then to us by the will of God. This exceeded the hope of St. Paul for them. Perhaps all he hoped for or expected from them was just to send part of their money to the poor in Jerusalem, but they actually went above and beyond: they gave themselves to God, they gave themselves to the apostles as the ministers of God—because they know that this is the will of God, that is why he said, "By the will of God." In obedience to the Lord, they gave themselves to God and to St. Paul and the apostles, and sent their gift (their money or their contribution) abundantly

to Jerusalem. Their donation began when they surrendered themselves to God first and to the apostles second (as his agents) doing this in obedience to the will of God.

**8:6** So we urged Titus, that as he had begun, so he would also complete this grace in you as well. Apparently when Titus went to Corinth he began the collection for the saints in Jerusalem, as St. Paul had commanded them in the first Letter to the Corinthians 16:1. Now, using the example of the Macedonians, St. Paul urged Titus to go in order to complete this ministry that he had started with them, and to complete it before the arrival of St. Paul. Here, St. Paul was calling the ministry, "the grace," because as I mentioned before, in order to give, you need to receive the grace of God; the grace of God will help you to be able to give.

**8:7** But as you abound in everything. St. Paul was telling them, "You have grown in so many virtues, so many gifts, and now in order to be complete, you need to also grow and to abound in this gift, the gift of giving, the grace of giving."

in faith. In faith" means in full confidence in God, in full belief of the truth.

**in speech.** Speech refers to the ability to instruct others, so you abounded in speech, you are able to teach and instruct others.

**in knowledge.** Your experiential knowledge of God and knowledge of the truth.

**in all diligence.** Diligence means the zeal, the readiness in doing every spiritual activity.

**and in your love for us—see that you abound in this grace also.** Their love was manifested by their readiness to obey the commandments and instructions of St. Paul to them. St. Paul was telling them, "As you abounded in faith, in speech, in knowledge, in diligence, in love for us, now is the time to abound in this grace—the grace of giving, so that you will be complete in everything." It is as if St. Paul was telling them that character is not complete without abounding in giving. After St. Paul gave them the example of the churches in Macedonia, he used the example of our Lord Jesus Christ as our pattern, how the Lord gave abundantly—not only gave us money and what we eat and what we drink, but He gave Himself on the Cross.

**8:8 I speak not by commandment.** St. Paul was telling them, "I am not giving you a commandment, I am not giving you an order, because your giving should be done freely, you should have the willingness to give. But if you give out of guilt, if you give out of compulsion, if you give by force, it is not giving."

**but I am testing the sincerity of your love by the diligence of others.** That is why he told them, "I speak not by commandment because I want your giving to be done willingly, and thus your giving will be blessed. But I am encouraging you and I am testing and examining the sincerity of your love by giving you the example of the churches in Macedonia. I am testing the sincerity of your love by the diligence of others. By showing you the diligence of others, by presenting to you the diligence of the churches in Macedonia, I am actually encouraging, testing, and examining your sincerity of love." Love is expressed in giving, "For God so loved the world that He gave His only begotten Son." If your love is sincere, you will be a giving person. That is why he said, "I am testing the sincerity of your love by the example of others, by the diligence of others, by the example of the Macedonian churches."

**8:9 For you know the grace of our Lord Jesus Christ.** Because the Law was given by Moses but the grace and truth was given by Jesus Christ. He is saying, "You know the grace that God gave us by His incarnation. This great gift that God gave us by His incarnation and His death on the Cross.".

**that though He was rich, yet for your sakes He became poor.** God is not only rich, but He is the source of all riches. God emptied Himself, He descended from heaven and became Man, leaving all the glory and all the riches in heaven. Although He was rich, yet for your sakes He became poor. Why did He become poor? To save us, for our sake, to redeem us—that is why He became poor.

**that you through His poverty might become rich.** God did this in order to give us from the heavenly riches. He became poor in order to make us (the poor) rich in the heavenly places. St. Paul was telling them, "After I gave you the example of the churches in Macedonia, I will now use the biggest motivator for us to give, which is the example of our Lord Jesus Christ. The Lord gave up all things for us. He became poor that we might be rich in heavenly riches. If He gave Himself up for us, what shall we give for Him?

**8:10** **And in this I give advice.** St. Paul was telling them, "I am not giving you an order, I am not giving you a commandment, but I am giving you advice." What is this advice? "It is to your advantage not only to be doing what you began and were desiring to do a year ago; but now you also must complete the doing of it"—this is his

advice. Many people when they give, they think that they are losing, but St. Paul is telling us, "No, actually, when you give, you will be blessed." If we encourage you to give, it is not because God cannot provide; believe me, God can provide for all the poor in all the world without any of us giving anything. So why does God encourage us to give? In order for us to be blessed.

**It is to your advantage not only to be doing what you began and were desiring to do a year ago.** Think about the widow and Elijah. Was it not to her advantage to give? If she had refused to give, she would have eaten the cake with her son and then she would have died. But because she gave abundantly, God blessed her, and the oil and the flour did not vanish from her house until the end of the famine. St. Paul told them, "Think about it this way: when you give, you do not lose, but you actually receive, so it is to your advantage." He told them, "It is to your advantage not only to be doing what you began and were desiring to do a year ago, when Titus visited you; the desire is not enough."

**8:11** **but now you also must complete the doing of it; that as there was a readiness to desire it, so there also may be a completion out of what you have.** Perhaps Titus had talked to them about giving and they told him, "Yes, we're willing to give." But

St. Paul told them, "No, the willingness and the desire is not enough, you need to put it into action." That is why he said to them in verse 11, "but now you also must complete the doing of it—you had desire, you were willing, now you must complete the doing of it. Willingness is not enough; as you willed, you have to do. As there was a readiness to will, let there be performance by giving out what you have. You also must complete the doing of it that as there was a readiness to desire it, so there also may be a completion out of what you have. As you had the desire to give and you were ready to give, now you actually need to complete this according to what you have, according to your ability." St. Paul spoke about three principles. The first principle is willingness, the desire. So, when you give, you need to give by your own willingness, by your own desire, freely, not out of compulsion, not out of embarrassment, not out of guilt, but because you want to give.

Secondly, giving is done according to your ability, or what is above and beyond your ability, as the church in Macedonia did. Here St. Paul was telling them, "Now I want you to give and to complete out of what you have; see what you have and give."

**8:12** **For if there is first a willing mind, it is accepted according to what one has, and not according to what he does not have.** If you have this willingness and if you have a willing mind, "it is accepted (God will accept your giving) according to what one has, and not according to what he does not have." God is expecting you to give from what you have, He will not ask you to give from what you do not have, because if you do not have, how can you give? But if you have two mites, give from the two mites. If you have a small amount of oil and a small amount of flour, give from what you have—"It is accepted according to what one has, and not according to what he does not have." The willing mind has been shown in the readiness to will, which is essential to its acceptance—the readiness, the willingness is essential for God to accept my gift. That is the first principle—the readiness, the willingness. The second principle is to give according to your ability. God accepts the gift and measures it according to your means, according to your ability.

**8:13** **For I do not mean that others should be eased and you burdened.** St. Paul is saying, "I am not asking only you to give and leaving the rest of the churches at ease." If all of us, brothers and sisters in Christ, hear about somebody in need, all of us should support and give. He said, "I wish that all churches would give according to what they have. I do not mean to burden you and that the other churches be at ease, or to burden you and the needy in Jerusalem will be at ease at your expense."

none will have excess; none will have excess and none will be in want or lack.

**8:14** **But by an equality, that now at this time your abundance may supply their lack, that their abundance also may supply your lack—that there may be equality.** That is the third principle. He was saying, "Now there is a lack in Jerusalem so let your abundance supply it, so that tomorrow, if you become in want or are lacking something and they are in abundance, then they must supply it for you tomorrow. Then there will be equality." Because the church is an assembly of loving brethren, if you are in need, I should support you, and if I am in need you should support me; that is the principle of equality.

**8:15** **As it is written, "He who gathered much had nothing left over, and he who gathered little had no lack."** This verse is from Exodus 16:18. St. Paul was telling them, "As it is written in Exodus, if a person gathers a lot, then he will not have leftovers, because he gave the extra to the poor. And if I gather little, I am not lacking anything, because those who gathered more, give me from their extra. When one lacks, others supply so that all may be equally provided for." If we have this brotherly love, then there will be this distribution of what we have, so that no saint, no believer will be in want and

**8:16-24** In the last part of this chapter, from verses 16 to 24, St. Paul starts to discuss the practical ways of sending their contribution or their gift to Jerusalem.

**8:16** **But thanks be to God who puts the same earnest care for you into the heart of Titus.** St. Paul was emphasizing that everything is the will of God in our hearts; God is the One who put the care in the heart of Titus, and so, Titus talked to them about their contribution to Jerusalem. If it is God who put this care in the heart of Titus then we should actually give thanks to whom? To God. That is why he said, "Thanks be to God who puts the same earnest care for you into the heart of Titus." When Titus encouraged them to give he was actually caring about them because it is to their advantage to give. Titus was now ready to return to Corinth - carrying this second Letter to help in this ministry of collecting the money for the saints. St. Paul said, "This was because of the grace of God because God put this earnest care in the heart of Titus."

**8:17 For he not only accepted the exhortation, but being more diligent, he went to you of his own accord.** St. Paul was telling them, "Titus is coming to you not because I commanded him, not because I asked him, but from himself—according to his own accord he wanted to go to you— it was his desire." Not only in giving does it have to come from our own desire, but also in serving. When we serve, we should not be serving out of compulsion or guilt or embarrassment, but we should serve out of our desire because we have the readiness and the willingness to serve. Not only did Titus readily accept the work that St. Paul suggested to him, but also out of his own accord he went to them for the collection for the saints. He desired to do this; he chose to do this.

**8:18 And we have sent with him the brother whose praise is in the gospel throughout all the churches.** St. Paul did not mention the name of this brother, but most scholars say that this brother is St. Luke. He sent another person with Titus, in fact, he actually sent three messengers: Titus is number one, St. Luke is number two. He said about St. Luke, "Whose praise is in the gospel throughout all the churches," because of his labor in the Gospel, maybe because he was writing both the Gospel of St. Luke as well as writing the Book of Acts, and perhaps, also because he participated in preaching the Gospel of salvation. He said, "We did not send Titus only but we sent with him Luke, whose praise is in the Gospel, in the preaching of the Gospel. He is praised because he is preaching the Gospel throughout all the churches." ❧ In dealing with money, it is usually better that it is not just one person dealing with the money. Even if he is very faithful, if only one person is dealing with the money, this may give opportunity for people to falsely accuse him. Even so it was with Titus, Paul, Luke and Apollos, as we are going to see, he did not send Titus by himself but three persons. This is why in the churches we usually emphasize that all the checks should be signed by two persons, that the collection of donations should be done by at least two or three persons. This is a Biblical principle from the teaching of St. Paul as he said, "We want to be in honor before God and before men. We do not want anyone to falsely accuse us or question our integrity and our faithfulness."

**8:19 and not only that, but who was also chosen by the churches to travel with us with this gift, which is administered by us.** "And not only that"—not only that his praise is throughout all the churches— he is still speaking about St. Luke—"but who was also chosen by the churches." The churches in Macedonia chose St. Luke, "to travel with us with this gift"— so they entrusted St. Luke with their contribution and to travel with them with this gift to Jerusalem, "which is administered by us"—we are the ones who are administrating, coordinating the collection of the money to be sent to Jerusalem. But why are we doing this? The next segment of the verse explains: "...to the glory of the Lord"

**to the glory of the Lord Himself.** We have organized it and it is administrated by us, "to the glory of the Lord Himself." We did not lose our focus. Our focus, while we are collecting the money is to glorify God, so we are careful how we administer, we are careful in every step while we are collecting this money. ⚜ The main goal is not only to provide for the needy, but for God to be glorified. Everything we do, we should do for the glory of the Lord. That is why if in the process of helping the needy, you do not glorify God, it is not right. I heard about an organization that, in order to collect money for the poor, invited an actress  and held an auction for her jewelry; this is against glorifying God. When we collect, we have to do it for the glory of the Lord.

**to show your ready mind.** St. Paul is saying, "We want to show your readiness to others, to show that you have the zeal and the desire and the willingness to help your brethren in Jerusalem." St. Luke was appointed by the churches of Macedonia to carry their gift from Macedonia to Jerusalem, and another purpose of why he was sending St. Luke in in order to "stir up

their ready mind," to make their ready mind known and manifest to others, to make others know how readily and freely they came into this service.

**8:20** **avoiding this: that anyone should blame us in this lavish gift which is administered by us.** "We are very careful for this to be for the glory of God. We were very careful not to give reason to anyone to blame us, not to give reason for anyone to say that we used this money to our advantage or that we took part of the money for ourselves. That is why I did not deal with the money personally, but I sent the three brethren—Titus, St. Luke, and the third brother, Apollos; I actually did not send one person. I sent three of them because they had a lot of money collected." He did not want anyone to speak negatively or to question their integrity, lest some persons would charge them that St. Paul used the gift for his own advantage. The messengers, these three persons, would report how the funds were used.

**8:21** **Providing honorable things, not only in the sight of the Lord, but also in the sight of men.** Just because we are leaders in the church we cannot just say, "You know, I am faithful. Let people say whatever they want to say." Because I am a leader, my mistakes will offend many people; that is why I should be very, very careful lest I offend someone. Why did St. Paul say, "We want to provide honorable things, we want to provide an honorable image, not only in the sight of God — God searches our hearts and our kidneys; God knows exactly who we are—but also in the sight of men. Taking care to act so that we are not only cleared in the sight of God but also cleared in the sight of all men, and avoiding even the appearance of evil, because if St. Paul had taken the money by himself, one might have said, "He took this money for himself." He was extremely careful not to give any reason for anyone to question his integrity.

**8:22 And we have sent with them our brother whom we have often proved diligent in many things, but now much more diligent, because of the great confidence which we have in you.** "And we have sent with them"—with Luke and Titus, "our brother"—that is the third one, Apollos, "whom we have often proved diligent in many things, but now much more diligent, because of the great confidence which we have in you." St. Paul said that the third person was Apollos. He did not mention his name but again, the scholars and commentators of the Scriptures said that most probably this was Apollos. Why did they choose Apollos? He said that they chose Apollos because he was very diligent in many things. "But when Apollos knew your

confidence in us, and how much you love us and obey our commandments, he became more diligent and committed to this service more than he had already been." It is as if St. Paul was telling them, "When Apollos found that I have the fullest confidence in your love for me, he engaged in this service with enthusiasm, with diligence that even exceeded his former diligence. He became more diligent than before."

**8:23 If anyone inquires about Titus, he is my partner and fellow worker concerning you.** If anyone inquires about who Titus is, "he is my partner and fellow worker concerning you." It is like he is giving a recommendation letter. "If anyone asks who Titus is, he is my companion, he is my fellow laborer, he is working for you, he is serving you." Titus was a disciple of St. Paul, but do you see the humbleness of St. Paul? He called Titus his companion.

**Or if our brethren are inquired about, they are messengers of the churches, the glory of Christ.** "Our brethren" refers to Luke and Apollos. If somebody asks or questions who Luke and Apollos are, "they are messengers of the churches." Messengers means apostles of the church. "The glory of Christ"—they are actually doing this service so that Christ may be glorified. What a wonderful testimony about Titus, Luke, and Apollos! Who are these brethren? They are the apostles of the churches, promoting the glory of Christ.

**8:24    Therefore show to them, and before the churches, the proof of your love and of our boasting on your behalf.** Since these are the delegates of the churches, since these are the apostles and the messengers of Christ, receive them warmly, receive them with love, show them and the other churches—like the churches of Macedonia showed you—your love toward us. This will be the proof of your love toward us. Give proof of your love, and show that when we have boasted of your excellences, that our boasting was not in vain. If our boasting were in vain, it would create a negative reputation for these churches in Corinth, and on me personally. St. Paul told them, "Now knowing that these are the apostles and the messengers of Christ promoting the glory of God, receive them warmly and show them the evidence, the proof, of your love to God, to the poor, to me, and also show them that our boasting in you (what we said about you) was true and was not a lie or in vain."

## Chapter 8 Questions

1. What was the condition of the churches in Macedonia? Yet what did they have in abundance?

2. What three things are said in how they gave?

3. How did they go beyond St. Paul's expectations?

4. Why did St. Paul send Titus?

5. What two examples did St. Paul use motivate them to give?

6. What three guidelines does St. Paul give to govern their giving?

7. What three men were sent to administer this collection?

8. Why were these men handling the collection, and not St. Paul?

9. What did St. Paul want the Corinthians to show to these men and the other churches?

# 9

## Chapter Outline

- Administering the Gift (1-5)
- The Cheerful Giver (6-15)

**9:1** **Now concerning the ministering to the saints, it is superfluous for me to write to you.** St. Paul calls the poor "the saints," so when he says "ministering to the saints," he means to serve the poor, support them, supply their needs. Why does St. Paul consider it to be superfluous for him to write about ministering to the saints? Because they had already started collecting for the poor one year ago, St. Paul feels that he does not need to write more. They were fully instructed and had already begun the work of collection for the poor, so he was telling them, "It is superfluous for me to write to you."

**9:2** **For I know your willingness, about which I boast of you.** St. Paul was explaining why he felt it was not necessary to write about collections; he told them, "For I know your willingness, I know your readiness, that is why it seemed to me unnecessary to write to you about collections." St. Paul actually used the churches at Corinth as an example to the Macedonians, telling them, "See how the churches in Corinth collected this money for the poor?"

**to the Macedonians, that Achaia was ready a year ago.** He was referring to the churches which were in the province of Achaia, of which Corinth was the capital—"that Achaia was ready a year ago"—so they had actually begun the collection one year prior.

**and your zeal has stirred up the majority.** When St. Paul used the Corinthians as an example, this motivated many other churches to collect money and send it to the poor. As he said, "And your zeal has stirred up the majority"—motivated the majority, in order to raise some money and send it to the poor.

**9:3** **Yet I have sent the brethren, lest our boasting of you should be in vain in this respect, that, as I said, you may be ready.** Here he spoke about the brethren mentioned in Chapter 8 (St. Luke, Titus, and Apollos). St. Paul was now explaining why he sent the brethren. If they were ready or they had started the work one year ago (maybe they started but did not continue) St. Paul was telling them, "I have already put you as an example and I boast about you before other churches, so now I want my boasting to not be in vain, that is why I sent the brethren in order that you complete the work that you had begun last year, and so that when I come to you, you will be ready." That is one reason why St. Paul was sending the brethren, in order to make them ready and to finish the work which they had started one year ago, so that his boasting about them before other churches would not be in vain.

**9:4    Lest if some Macedonians come with me and find you unprepared, we (not to mention you!) should be ashamed of this confident boasting.** St. Paul was telling them, "When I boast about you I boast with confidence, I am sure that you will be ready. But let us assume that you did not finish the ministry that you started one year ago and you stopped collecting money for the poor, and most probably when I come to you some Macedonians will come with me, I will be embarrassed, not to mention that you will also be embarrassed. Because I boasted about you and I told them that you were ready since last year, so it will be as if my boasting about you was in vain, and so you and I will be ashamed." "Lest if some Macedonians come with me and find you unprepared, we (St. Paul), "(not to mention you!)"—and also you, "should be ashamed of this confident boasting"—that although we boasted about you with confidence, now we will be ashamed." He sent the three brethren so that they would surely be

prepared when he comes to them, and if the Macedonians should find Corinth unprepared with the collection when St. Paul comes, it would fill St. Paul and the church in Corinth with shame.

**9:5    Therefore I thought it necessary to exhort the brethren to go to you ahead of time, and prepare your generous gift beforehand, which you had previously promised, that it may be ready as a matter of generosity and not as a grudging obligation.".** St. Paul was giving them another reason why he sent the brethren to collect the money; not only to be ready before the Macedonians and that his boasting about them would not be in vain, but: "that it may be ready as a matter of generosity and not as a grudging obligation." Some people give with cheerfulness, some people give because they want to give, but other people give because they are embarrassed; they feel obligated to give. St. Paul was saying, "God will not approve your giving if you give it out of obligation, if you give it out of compulsion, and then you complain about it," that is what he meant here by "grudging obligation." If St. Paul went to them and said, "I want to collect the money now!" then the people would start to collect, but maybe their giving would now be out of obligation, not happily, not cheerfully. ✤ That is why when Pope Shenouda became Patriarch he stopped this habit of collecting money in plates, because we actually embarrass the person when we present the plate to him to give his offering, because some people may give out of obligation, out of embarrassment, not because they want to give, and as St. Paul will explain, God loves a cheerful giver. ❖ Do not give out of compulsion, do not give out of obligation; do not give and afterwards complain. This is not only about money, but about any source of service. For example, if I come and ask you to do a certain service in the church and you do not have time to do it, or maybe you are not interested in this service, or maybe you simply just do not want to do it but you feel embarrassed because the priest asked you to do this service, so you do the service, but in the meantime you are complaining and doing it with grumbling, and grudgingly, St. Paul said that this is the wrong attitude. When you give, you need to give with generosity, not as a grudging obligation. He thought it necessary to send the brethren, that the work might surely be completed as an abundant gift, and not as an obligation done with complaints.

**9:6** **But this I say: He who sows sparingly will also reap sparingly, and he who sows bountifully will also reap bountifully.** From verse, St. Paul starts to explain the principle of the cheerful giver. St. Paul was saying that giving is like sowing. If you sow one seed then you will reap a small amount of fruit, but if you sow many seeds then you will reap much fruit, so whatever you sow you will reap. "And he who sows bountifully will also reap bountifully"—so whatever you give, God will bless based on how much you give. ❖ And here again, I am not only speaking about giving money, but any sort of service, any kind of giving you offer.

**9:7** **So let each one give as he purposes in his heart.** Again, St. Paul is reemphasizing the fact that you should not give out of compulsion or while complaining, grudgingly, because this attitude will not be accepted by God.

**not grudgingly or of necessity; for God loves a cheerful giver.** Necessity means with compulsion, you feel obligated to give; it should be as you purpose in your heart. What does he mean by "as you purpose in your heart?" Your heart should approve your giving first, and your heart should be happy about whatever you give first. Then if your heart is happy and you purpose to give, then however much you give will be pleasing to God because God loves a cheerful giver. The giving must be done cheerfully.

**9:8** **And God is able to make all grace abound toward you, that you, always having all sufficiency in all things, may have an abundance for every good work.** Here St. Paul was comparing giving with sowing. When the farmer sows the seed, who will make this seed grow and multiply and bear fruit? God. St. Paul was saying, "The same God who makes the seed grow, multiply, and increase, is able to make all grace abound toward you." When you give, God will bless you with every sort of blessing. God is able to bestow upon you every sort of blessing—temporal as well as spiritual, in this life here and in the life there. "And God is able to make all grace abound toward you, that you, always having all sufficiency in all things, may have an abundance for every good work." Why will God give you? St. Paul was saying that God will give you abundantly so that you will have sufficiency in everything. And when you have sufficiency in everything you will give more; you will have an abundance for every good work, you will have extra money to better help the poor. ❋ Let me say it this way: if God sees that you have a kind heart and you help the poor generously, then God will give you more because you already have a kind heart and you will help more. And God is now sure that if He gives you, you will spend it on the poor, so God will not hesitate to give you more and more, because you are generous. But if God sees you stingy in your giving (you do not give liberally

or with abundance) then God will not entrust you with more money because He will say, "If I give him more money he will keep the money for himself, he will not distribute it to the poor." St. Paul was saying that God is able to make all grace abound toward you. God is able to bless you with every sort of blessing—blessed is a cheerful giver—so that when you have sufficiency in everything you may abound in every good deed, in every good work; any opportunity, you will abound in it. ❋ We actually quote this message in the Divine Liturgy of the Coptic Orthodox Church, in the Litany of the Waters, the Wind & the Seed—we ask that having sufficiency in everything, we may abound in every good deed. "Always having all sufficiency in all things, may have an abundance for every good work." The faithful steward will be trusted with more.

**9:9** **As it is written.** Written in Psalm 112:9. This Psalm starts with, "Blessed is the man who fears the Lord."

**He has dispersed abroad, He has given to the poor; His righteousness endures forever.** In this Psalm, David speaks about the man who fears the Lord, and this man does not hold tightly but dispenses abroad by giving to the poor. Because God sees this person giving abundantly to the poor, God will also give him abundantly so that his righteousness—and what does he mean here by 'his righteousness?' The righteous acts, the righteous deeds in giving to the poor, so that his righteousness may endure forever. God supplies him with many blessings in order to keep his righteousness, in order to support the virtue of giving to the poor.

**9:10  Now may He who supplies seed to the sower, and bread for food.** In other words: "It is God who supplies the seed to the sower. As God gives the seed to the farmer to sow, God gives also you the money in order to plant and distribute to the poor. God gives bread for food and in the same way He gives us money to help others with this money."

**supply and multiply the seed you have sown and increase the fruits of your righteousness.** May God "supply and multiply the seed you have sown"—your contribution that you sent to Jerusalem, "and increase the fruits of your righteousness"—which means that God will give you more and more, in order that you, in the future, may give more and more abundantly.

**9:11  while you are enriched in everything for all liberality.** God will give you abundantly while you are enriched in everything for all liberality.

God will make you rich in everything— rich in virtue, rich financially, rich spiritually. And here financially does not mean that you will be a billionaire, but to have enough to give to the poor, and to be content and happy.

**which causes thanksgiving.** Your generous giving will cause the poor to give thanks to God! You are not only giving the poor, but you are motivating them to praise the Lord, glorify His name, and give thanks to Him. As they are enriched, their giving will be with liberality, when God enriches them, their giving will be abundant, and this will cause thanksgiving to God on the part of the recipients—the poor.

**through us to God.** St. Paul says "through us" because St. Paul coordinated it; he was the servant who collected the money from Corinth and sent it to Jerusalem. It is like any service committee; they coordinate, they take the money from here and send it there. St. Paul said, "These people who take the money from here and send it there actually glorify God, because when they send the money there, they supply these people needs and motivate them to give thanks to the Lord."

**9:12    For the administration of this service not only supplies the needs of the saints, but also is abounding through many thanksgivings to God.** Two things resulted from your generous giving. Number one—the needs of the poor are supplied; number two—their thanksgiving to God increased, became abundant." ❖ I usually say to the social service committees that there is a big difference between serving in a social service committee and serving in any philanthropic society. Any philanthropic society or committee serves only to supply the needs of people, that is why many of these societies are Atheist. But for a Christian committee that helps the poor, this committee's goal should be glorifying God and giving thanks to God; there is a big difference between a philanthropic society helping the poor and a church helping the poor. When a church helps the poor, they should not only be supplying needs but should also be giving thanks to God and glorifying God. ❖ That is why the way we collect the money for the poor should be right. Glorifying God means using the proper ways of collecting money and the proper ways of distributing the money.

**9:13 while, through the proof of this ministry, they glorify God.** When St. Paul says "they" he was not referring to the poor. Rather, he was speaking about some Christian Jews (Christian, from Jewish background) who attacked the Gentiles. They were questioning and casting doubts as to whether the churches of the Gentiles are churches of Christ or not. St. Paul was saying, "There are two more

blessings in sending this money to the poor in Jerusalem (for a total of four blessings). The first blessing is that you will supply the needs of the poor, the second blessing is that they will give thanks to God because of your generosity; number three, when the Judaizers (the Christians from Jewish background who were attacking the Gentiles) hear about how the church in Corinth is supporting—in love and in generosity—the church in Jerusalem which is a Jewish church, or rather, a Christian church of Jewish background, then they will know that they are following the same Gospel (the Gospel of Christ) and will glorify God and their false accusations against the Gentile churches will stop. What he was saying here is, "Through the proof of this ministry, when they see how generously you give in order to support your brethren in Jerusalem"—and why did the Jews in Jerusalem become their brethren? Because now, in Christ, the Jews and Gentiles became one; we became one in the cross of the Lord Jesus Christ. That is why the Gentiles are now supporting the Jews.

**for the obedience of your confession to the gospel of Christ, and for your liberal sharing with them and all men.** They will know that your faith, your confession, is obedient to the Gospel of Christ who said, "I was hungry and you gave Me food, I was thirsty and you gave Me drink, I was naked and you clothed Me," and for your liberal sharing with them and with all men, because you give with generosity, not only to them but to everybody." That is the third blessing, and such a gift would tend to open the minds of the Judaizers and to remove their prejudice, and they would admit that the Corinthians are subject to the Gospel of Christ.

**9:14    and by their prayer for you, who long for you because of the exceeding grace of God in you.** He is saying, "You will motivate the Judaizers to not only stop attacking you, but also to pray for you while longing to see you, in order to see the grace of God that is abundant in you." "So, the Judaizers, filled with affection for you and longing for you on account of the proof of God's grace to you, will glorify God by praying for you." This is the fourth blessing. The Judaizers will not only be in peace with the Gentiles, but they will also be longing to go see them, meet them, and pray to God on their behalf.

**9:15    Thanks be to God for His indescribable gift!.** As you know, St. Paul struggled much with the Judaizers, and many people accused him of defiling the Temple because he was preaching to the Gentiles, but now St. Paul saw how God united the Gentiles and the Jews together in Christianity. That is why he ended the chapter by giving praise to

the Lord. He said, "This gift, the grace of salvation, the Cross which united the heavenly with the earthly, united the Jews with the Gentiles, united man with himself, this gift is indescribable. No one, no tongue, and no language can express the depth of this gift. That is why he said, "Thanks be to God," St. Paul burst out in thanksgiving to God for His gift, the gift of salvation, which no language can describe, which broke down the enmity between the Jews and Gentiles and made them one in Christ.

## Chapter 9 Questions

1. What three guidelines does St. Paul give to govern their giving?

2. What three men were sent to administer this collection?

3. Why were these men handling the collection, and not St. Paul?

4. What did St. Paul want the Corinthians to show to these men and the other churches?

# 10

## Chapter Outline

- The Spiritual War (1-6)
- Reality of St. Paul's Authority (7-11)
- Limits of St. Paul's Authority (12-18)

and very kind when he was in Corinth, but after he had left Corinth and heard about the person who committed sexual immorality and sinned with his father's wife, he had sent them a very harsh letter and excommunicated this man, as we read in first Corinthians 5. So, they were saying and accusing him, that in his letters he was very bold and harsh but in presence he was lowly and meek.

**10:1  Now I, Paul, myself am pleading with you by the meekness and gentleness of Christ.** Here, St. Paul did not mention any of his fellow workers; in the beginning he spoke in plural, but now he is using the singular. He was using a tone of severity. We might wonder why. Since the opposition and the false accusations were directed at him personally, he is speaking in the singular and starting to defend himself. But while defending himself and using a severe tone, he is trying to keep the balance between severity and the meekness and gentleness of Christ. He does not want to be overtaken by severity to the point where he loses his meekness and gentleness.

**who in presence am lowly among you, but being absent am bold toward you.** St. Paul was reminding them of the accusation: "You are saying that in my presence I am lowly among you, that when I am present I am actually weak, but when I am absent I am harsh and bold toward you." His opponents said that he was very gentle

**10:2  But I beg you that when I am present I may not be bold with that confidence by which I intend to be bold against some, who think of us as if we walked according to the flesh.** St. Paul was addressing another accusation here; they accused him of walking according to the flesh. Walking according to the flesh means that he is led by worldly motives. St. Paul was telling them, "When I come, I have confidence that I can use my authority and be bold and be harsh with those who think of me as if I am walking according to the flesh, but I am begging you, I am pleading with you to repent so that when I come to you I may not use this boldness. I do not want my visit with you to be a harsh one in which I am bold and severe with these false teachers." He was asking them, so that when he comes he may not have to exercise that boldness which he feared that he might need to use to admonish some of the opponents if they do not repent, because they accused him of being led by worldly motives.

**10:3    For though we walk in the flesh, we do not war according to the flesh.** Now he was defending against the second accusation by saying, "Although I am still in the body, although I am still in the flesh, I do not use carnal weapons in my warfare, I do not war according to the flesh."

**10:4    For the weapons of our warfare are not carnal but mighty in God for pulling down strongholds.** Our enemy is Satan and all his soldiers. Since our enemy is not a carnal being but a spiritual being, our weapons of warfare are spiritual, are not carnal. These weapons are strong in God, who gave us the power and the authority to overcome all the difficulties, to overcome all the obstacles, to pull down strongholds and to defeat our enemy, the devil." This gives us hope. Many of us think that our repentance is difficult, we fall in the same sin over and over, we cannot defeat sins in our life. The reason for this is that we are not putting on the whole armor of God, or perhaps we are using carnal weapons, not spiritual weapons. If you are captive to a certain sin, if you are like a captive in one of these strongholds of Satan, if you use your spiritual weapons, these spiritual weapons are mighty in God and able to pull down strongholds and to release you from the captivity of Satan.

**10:5    casting down arguments and every high thing that exalts itself against the knowledge of God.** The spiritual weapons are the word of God, prayer, the sacraments of the Church, spiritual readings, all these spiritual weapons are able to destroy all vain reasoning and all human philosophy against the knowledge of God. Any argument against the knowledge of God could be destroyed by the spiritual weapons. Any ideology, any philosophy, any human wisdom that exalts itself and makes a barrier against the knowledge of God, our spiritual weapons can actually destroy. Not only that, but "bringing every thought into captivity to the obedience of Christ."

**bringing every thought into captivity to the obedience of Christ.** Instead of being captive to our thoughts, now, by using the spiritual weapons, I will be able to take every thought that attacks me captive to the obedience of Christ, which means I can overcome all the evil thoughts. I can overcome all the blaspheming thoughts, any thought casting doubt on God, any thought casting doubt on the Scripture. By using the spiritual weapons, I am able to do three things: (1) pull down strongholds, to release myself from the captivity of sin, (2) destroy all arguments and all philosophies against the knowledge of God, (3) bring into captivity every thought to the obedience of Christ, to bring the faculty of the mind into the obedience of Christ by overcoming all the blaspheming and evil thoughts.

**10:6  nd being ready to punish all disobedience.** Not only are the spiritual weapons able to pull down strongholds and to destroy every thought that exalts itself against the knowledge of Christ, and to bring every thought into captivity to the obedience of Christ, but also (number four)—the spiritual weapons are ready and do enable the apostles and those who are in authority to punish all disobedience. St. Paul was telling them, "I have the authority, I have the sacrament of priesthood by which I can punish all disobedient in Corinth."

**when your obedience is fulfilled.** St. Paul said, "I will give you time to repent so that when the faithful give proof of their obedience, when your obedience is fulfilled,  I will come and discipline and rebuke and punish only the disobedient. If I am waiting, I am waiting lest I punish the innocent with the guilty. If I am waiting, I am waiting in order to give you opportunity to show me your obedience, in order to know who is obedient and who is not, who is faithful and who is not. After your obedience is fulfilled, I will use the spiritual weapons to punish the unfaithful and the disobedient." By this point, St. Paul had completely responded to the accusation that he was walking according to the flesh. He told them, "Yes, I am still living in the flesh but I am not walking according to the flesh and I am not using carnal weapons, but spiritual weapons."

**10:7  Do you look at things according to the outward appearance? If anyone is convinced in himself that he is Christ's, let him again consider this in himself, that just as he is Christ's, even so we are Christ's.** St. Paul was asking them, "Do any of you judge the apostle of Christ, the minister of Christ, the servant of Christ, by his person or by the outward circumstances? How do you evaluate us?" That is why he told them, "Do you look at things according to the outward appearance? When I came to you I was gentle and kind—does this mean that I have no authority and am not a true apostle? This judgement is according to outward appearance. I was kind and gentle with you to give you an opportunity to repent, and now will you use this to say that I am not an apostle?" "Let me tell you, if anyone is convinced that he is a servant of Christ or belonging to Christ, let him know—and I am saying this gently now, because when I come I will punish him and show him my authority that he may learn that I am also an apostle of Christ. Let him learn by himself before I come and convince him by a more severe method, by discipline and punishment, that we too belong to Christ. If the false teachers claim to be Christ's, I also have an equal claim; I also belong to Christ."

**10:8** **For even if I should boast somewhat more about our authority, which the Lord gave us for edification and not for your destruction, I shall not be ashamed.** He was telling them, "If you want to compare my privileges and my authority which were given to me by God, I will not be ashamed. If you want to evaluate me, it should not be according to the outward appearance, but if you use right measures to evaluate me, to examine my ministry, to examine my service, to examine the fruits of my preaching, I will not be ashamed. I want to tell you why I was gentle: because the authority that God gave me was given for edification and not for destruction; I understand that this authority was given to me to save and edify, not to destroy." This is a teaching for all of us. If you are in authority, whether as a clergy, Sunday school servant, deacon coordinator, or if you are in authority at your home (as parents or as a husband) or if you have authority at your work (as a manager or as a leader) or in any capacity, you should learn that God gave you the authority for edification and not for destruction. Many people actually abuse their authority, and instead of edifying the people, they destroy them. St. Paul was very aware that this authority was given to him for edification and not for destruction. Now he was again responding to the first accusation (why he was kind, why he appeared to be weak or having no authority), it was because he was trying to help them, to save them. He did not want to discipline, punish, and excommunicate, but he wanted to save them and help them.

**10:9** **lest I seem to terrify you by letters.** He was saying, "I am saying this lest I should seem like a parent terrifying his children with empty threats and no action." Do you know how a parent might sometimes yell at his son or daughter and threaten them, but when it comes to reality, they do nothing? St. Paul was saying, "Now I want you to know that these are not empty threats, I am not sending you this letter just to terrify you. I want you to know that I am very serious; when I come this time, I will punish and discipline those who are disobedient and unfaithful."

**10:10** **"For his letters."** St. Paul used the plural here because although this is the second Letter, all the scholars say that there was another letter sent to the Corinthians before this second Letter, but that letter is lost. So, we have the first Letter and the second Letter and in-between these two there is a missing letter that he sent to them, but unfortunately it was not saved for us.

**they say, "are weighty and powerful, but his bodily presence is weak, and his speech contemptible."** He is reminding them of the accusations:

"Many of you say, 'There was no authority in his manner,' but that when I am present among you I am kind, meek, and gentle, while in the meantime, the false teachers, in presence, speak with authoritarian language." St. Paul told them, "No, this time when I come, I will show you my authority in Christ."

**10:11** **Let such a person consider this, that what we are in word by letters when we are absent, such we will also be in deed when we are present.** He was telling them, "Let all who make such accusations about me know that when I come this time, I will be in presence exactly as my letters. You say my letters are strong, harsh, mighty, weighty, powerful— when I come this time, I want you to know that my presence will be exactly the same."

**10:12** **For we dare not class ourselves or compare ourselves with those who commend themselves.** Many times St. Paul used irony or sarcasm, and in this verse when he said "we dare not," he was saying, "I do not dare to class myself or to compare myself with the false teachers who commend themselves." This indicates sarcasm or irony; he is sarcastically saying, "I do not dare to associate myself, to class myself, or to compare myself with these false teachers who

commend and praise themselves."

**But they, measuring themselves by themselves, and comparing themselves among themselves, are not wise.** Now the tone changed from irony to seriousness. He was saying, "These false teachers, instead of measuring themselves by the public's standard or according to the Law of God, measure themselves by their own measure!" And when they compare themselves, they compare themselves to one another, not to others who excel them or others who are superior to them, but they compare themselves to those who are similar to them or inferior to them. Although they claim to be wise, yet in measuring themselves to themselves and comparing themselves to themselves, they prove to be unwise. This is a very unwise practice—to set the measure or standard, and then evaluate and compare myself with those who are similar to me, or inferior to me.

**10:13** **We, however, will not boast beyond measure, but within the limits of the sphere which God appointed us—a sphere which especially includes you.** St. Paul was addressing a third accusation. The first accusation was that his letters are strong but his presence is weak. The second accusation was that he walks according to the flesh. The third accusation was that he extended himself beyond the measure, beyond the sphere that God appointed for him. For example, if a priest is responsible for a certain city and he goes beyond this certain city, it is as if he extended himself beyond the area which was appointed to him by God. They said that when St. Paul went to Corinth, he extended himself beyond the area that God had appointed for him. He was saying two things: number one—we will not boast beyond measure which means that I will not evaluate myself and say that I am perfect, since I would be setting the measures by which I examine myself. There is no limit to one's high opinion of himself as long as he measures himself by himself and does not compare himself with his superiors. St. Paul was saying, "I will not do this, I will not boast beyond measure. I will not say, "I am so and so and so and so," when in reality I am not all of those things." Number two— "I will not extend myself beyond my boundaries, beyond my limits, beyond the sphere which God appointed for me to preach the Gospel and to labor within, for the Gospel. We will not, like them, boastfully extend ourselves beyond our boundary and our limit, because St. Paul's measure or standard is the appointment and choosing of God. God appointed to him a certain sphere to which he should preach the Gospel and St. Paul respected this. mentioned previously, the false teachers, the Judaizers, said that St. Paul had exceeded his authority in coming to Corinth, when actually, he went to Corinth based on the appointment of the Holy Spirit. In Acts 16:9 you will see that the Holy Spirit actually moved them to go and preach the Gospel in Europe. And the Apostles told them (at the Council of Jerusalem) that Peter will be an apostle for the Jews and Paul would be an apostle to the Gentiles, and Corinth was a Gentile city. So, when he went to Corinth, he went according to the appointment of God and the Holy Spirit. In Romans, St. Paul made it very clear that his way of preaching was to never go to a place where someone had preached before him. It was St. Paul's way to preach only where no one before him had preached the Gospel, and he mentioned this clearly in his letter to the Romans.

**10:14** **For we are not overextending ourselves (as though our authority did not extend to you), for it was to you that we came with the gospel of Christ.** He said, "When we came to you, you are part of our authority; this sphere includes you. Thus, when we came to you, we were not overextending ourselves, as if our authority did not include you or did not extend to you. It was to you that we came with the gospel of Christ, it was to you that God sent me to preach the Gospel."

**10:15** **not boasting of things beyond measure, that is, in other men's labors.** He was saying, "I am not boasting in other people's or other apostles' services. For example, if Peter preached in an area and then I came in and claimed that I preached in this area and took the credit, this would be wrong. I am not boasting of things beyond measure, meaning, in other men's labor, like the false teachers"— because St. Paul founded the church in Corinth, but the false teachers said, "We founded the church at Corinth." St. Paul was saying, "I am not doing this, I am not preaching, I am not boasting in another man's labor. My hope was that if your faith is increasing and you are steadfast in your faith, then I could go beyond Corinth to preach the Gospel into other cities of the Gentiles, outside Corinth. But now, because of all these problems and all this tension, it is as if you are hindering me from going beyond the sphere of Corinth."

**but having hope, that as your faith is increased, we shall be greatly enlarged by you in our sphere.** If your faith is growing, we shall be greatly enlarged. The sphere of preaching will be greatly enlarged by you when you help me in your sphere, so we can go beyond Corinth. His hope was that his success in Corinth and the support of the church there would enable him to carry the Gospel beyond Corinth; to preach the Gospel in the region beyond Corinth, where no man had yet preached.

**10:16** **to preach the gospel in the regions beyond you, and not to boast in another man's sphere of accomplishment.** In other words, "This was my hope; I wanted to preach the Gospel in the regions beyond you, and not to boast in another man's sphere of accomplishment—as I will not boast in the accomplishments of another apostle. As I told you, I will not claim that I preached to a city when that city was preached to by St. Peter or St. John or St. Matthew, so I refuse to boast in another man's sphere of accomplishment."

**10:17** **But "he who glories, let him glory in the Lord."** St. Paul is quoting from Jeremiah 9:23—He who glories, let him glory in the LORD. Here he is giving the true rule of boasting: we boast only in God, we do not boast in our own accomplishments or in ourselves, but as written in Jeremiah, let the Lord be our boast, our glory, for we are nothing, he who glories, let him glory in the LORD.

**10:18** **For not he who commends himself is approved, but whom the Lord commends.** If you praise yourself, this does not mean you are approved, but it is only if God commends you; if God praises you, you will be approved. The false teachers were boasting in another man's accomplishment, they were boasting in Corinth as if they preached to Corinth, although it was St. Paul who was the one who preached to Corinth. ❖ St. Paul was giving them advice and this advice is beneficial to every servant, every disciple, every deacon, every clergy, every teacher: let our work and life speak for us, not our lips. We should not praise ourselves; we should not commend ourselves.

**approved.** This means the one who will stand the test of the final trial, the one who will be approved in the final day, the one who will stand the test of faith or of the spiritual warfare. If you say, "I am strong, I can stand all the attacks of Satan," this will not commend you. But what will commend you is if God said, "Yes, you are worthy, you are approved, you are strong, you are spiritual." The approved one is the one commended or praised by the Lord, not the one who praises himself.

## Chapter 10 Questions

1. St. Paul said in verse 3, "For though we walk in the flesh, we do not war after the flesh." So how do we fight against the evil?

2. How did St. Paul describe the weapons of our warfare?

3. To what, we bring into captivity every thought?

4. The authority given to St. Paul is for edification or destruction?

5. In whom should we glory?

# 11

**11:1    Oh, that you would bear with me in a little folly.** The criticism of the false teachers made it necessary for St. Paul to defend himself. But St. Paul who had learned self-denial, who forgot himself completely for the sake of Christ and consecrated himself to God, when he defended himself and when he boasted, did this with a sense of shame. That is why he told them, "Oh, that you would bear with me in a little folly." He was apologizing for doing so, but he felt compelled to defend himself. It was as if he was saying to them, "I wish you to bear with me a little further while I enter at large into self-commendation."

**and indeed you do bear with me.** "Bear with me," as in, "Okay, if you consider it foolishness, bear with me, I want to defend myself to protect your faith," as he would later explain.

**11:2    For I am jealous for you with godly jealousy. For I have betrothed you to one husband, that I may present you as a chaste virgin to Christ.** "Why do I want to defend myself? What is the purpose of my ministry? My own glory? Never. The purpose of ministry is to bring you to Christ, unite you with Christ. Christ is the bridegroom and you are his bride, so when I baptized you I actually betrothed you to one Husband—Christ, but I want to present you as a chaste virgin, with no corruption of mind, with no corruption in the faith. If these false teachers succeed in accusing me (and you believe them), and then you start to stray away from the truth that I preached to you, you will be corrupted in your mind and faith and I cannot present you as a chaste virgin to Christ. This is why I am full of jealousy. I am jealous for you but not in a bad way; it is godly jealousy." The reason behind defending himself was not on behalf of himself, but on behalf of Christ. He betrothed them to Christ, the Bridegroom, and they are the bride. He had fear in his heart lest this bride may be led astray by the false teachers.
✢    In the Jewish tradition, marriage goes through three steps. The first step is engagement, the second step is betrothal, and the third step is marriage itself (the wedding). Engagement is a promise to marry, while betrothal is like the civil marriage—that is why here he calls Christ "Husband." It is a civil marriage but not yet consummated. But because it is a civil marriage, the wife

here (and I call her "wife," although they are not yet physically one) she is eligible for all the privileges of a wife. The consummation of the marriage, which is the wedding, is the third step. By the way, St. Mary was betrothed to St. Joseph, that is why when the angel said to Joseph, "Do not be afraid to take Mary, your wife," this wording is correct because she was legally his wife, although they never lived together as husband and wife. This marriage was not consummated, but she was legally his wife and was eligible for all the legal privileges. When a person hears about Christ and believes in Christ, that is the engagement. When you hear about Christ, it is as if Christ is proposing to you to accept Him as your Bridegroom, and if you believe in Christ and accept Him, this is the engagement. Then, when you are baptized and die with Christ and rise again, and are confirmed by the Holy Oil and partake of the sacrament of the Body and Blood of our Lord Jesus Christ, this is the betrothal. And now because we are the wife of the Son, we can call His Father our Father, and we can call God the Father, "Our Father who art in heaven." But before baptism a person cannot call God "our Father." Then when a person dies and goes to heaven, in the second coming of Christ, that is the actual consummation of the marriage. That is why we read in the Book of Revelation of the supper of the wedding of the Lamb. This helps explain to us the verse, "He who is born of God cannot sin," because many question saying, "We are children of

God yet we sin, so how is it that St. John said in his letter "he who is born of God cannot sin?" Yes, because the full adoption will happen after the wedding in the second coming of Christ, but now we are only betrothed to Him. When we become fully adopted, when the wedding happens, when the consummation, when the full union with Christ happens in His second coming, then we become fully adopted by God the Father, and it is only here that we cannot sin. That is why in Romans St. Paul said, "We are eagerly waiting for the adoption," and he explained the adoption as the redemption of our bodies. And the redemption of our bodies happens in the second coming of Christ, so yes, now we are betrothed and we are legally considered His children (the children of the Father) but we will be fully children in the second coming of Christ when our bodies are redeemed, and with the full adoption we cannot sin, as St. John said, "He who is born of the Father cannot sin." St. Paul told them, "I am defending myself and I will act foolishly by defending myself not for my own sake, but in order to present you as a chaste bride to Christ with no corruption of faith, with no corruption of mind, but if you follow the false teachers, they will corrupt your mind."

**11:3 But I fear, lest somehow, as the serpent deceived Eve by his craftiness, so your minds may be corrupted.** He told them, "Recall our mother, Eve, and how the serpent was able to deceive her and corrupt her mind by the craftiness of Satan. In the same way, I am afraid that your minds may be corrupted from the simplicity of Christ." The power of Satan lies in his ability to deceive. If Satan lost his ability to deceive, he would be powerless. Satan uses craftiness in order to deceive, so St. Paul was telling them, "As our mother Eve was seduced by the serpent, so I am also afraid that you will be led away by the false teachers."

**from the simplicity that is in Christ.** This refers to their single-minded devotion to Christ. They believed in Him, accepted Him, devoted their life to Him, followed Him, consecrated themselves to Him in a simple way, but now these false teachers will corrupt their minds. Perhaps someone will argue saying, "What is the relationship between the serpent and the false teacher, between Satan and the false teacher?" St. Paul explains that they are the servants of Satan. As Satan is able to deceive, so his servants (the servants of Satan) are also able to deceive.

**11:4 For if he who comes preaches another Jesus whom we have not preached, or if you receive a different spirit which you have not received, or a different gospel which you have not accepted—you may well put up with it!.** St. Paul was saying, "If the false teachers come preaching another Jesus or preaching another gospel, or giving you another spirit than the Holy Spirit that you received from us, maybe it might make sense that you would listen to them, but actually they are not preaching a new Jesus or giving you a new spirit or a new gospel. It is the same Jesus, it is the same Spirit, it is the same Gospel but in a corrupted way." These false teachers are called the "Judaizers." The Judaizers are false teachers from Jewish background who were teaching that unless you become Jewish and follow and keep the Law, you cannot be saved, so they are defiling the pure teaching of Christ, they are corrupting the pure teaching of Christ. Some scholars think that St. Paul used sarcasm in this verse. He told them, "The Judaizers perverted the Gospel so while it may look like another gospel, in reality it is not another gospel, it is not another Jesus, it is not another spirit, but it is a perverted form. They perverted the Gospel and at the same time discredited me, in order for you to not follow me nor follow the teaching that I gave you. What would be the result? You would follow the false teachers and then I could not present you as a chaste virgin to Christ."

**11:5** **For I consider that I am not at all inferior to the most eminent apostles.** Again, St. Paul is using sarcasm in this verse. These false teachers were describing themselves as "eminent apostles," so St. Paul was telling them, "I am not inferior to these eminent men who claim to be apostles"—of course they are not true apostles, but claimed that they are apostles of Christ and also claimed that they were eminent. St. Paul was telling them, "If I will compare myself with them, you will see that I am not at all inferior to them. No, actually, I am better than them, as I will explain."

**11:6** **Even though I am untrained in speech, yet I am not in knowledge. But we have been thoroughly manifested among you in all things.** St. Paul was very conscious that he was speaking to the Greeks (Corinth is a city in Greece). Greece was known for supremacy in speech, excellence of speech; all the philosophers came from Greece, like Socrates, Aristotle, and Plato. St. Paul told them, "I know myself; I am untrained in speech, I cannot use excellence of speech like the Greek philosophers, but I am not untrained in knowledge. I have the knowledge of Christ and I have the knowledge of truth, and this knowledge was actually thoroughly manifested among you in all things. Maybe I do not have the expressions of the Greek philosophers, but I am not lacking in Divine knowledge, and this knowledge has been manifested among you."

**11:7** **Did I commit sin in humbling myself ... because I preached the gospel of God to you free of charge?** The argument here is because he refused to take any financial support from them. The false teachers said, "He refused your gift (he refused your financial support) because he does not love you. He took from other churches but he did not take from you, this means he does not love you." St. Paul was stating a question here: "Did I commit sin in humbling myself, being humble among you and preaching the gospel of God to you free of charge? And why did I humble myself? So that you will be exalted when you believe in Christ. When I make your faith easy, without putting any burden on you (without asking you for any financial support) so that all you are to do is only believe in Christ—by making it easy for you to be exalted by believing in Christ, did I commit a sin? Because I preached the Gospel of God to you free of charge?" When he was there, he supported himself by his own labor. He worked with his own hand in order to support himself as we read in Acts 18:3. But these false apostles seemed to have charged money from them, versus St. Paul who did not dare ask for support. They told them, "We love you more than St. Paul, that is why we accept money from you."

**that you might be exalted.** He was referring to them being exalted by believing in Christ—when he preached the Gospel to them and they believed in Christ.

**11:8** **I robbed other churches, taking wages from them to minister to you.** St. Paul definitely needed financial support, so how was he able to preach to Corinth free of charge without getting any financial support from them? He was supported by other churches, other churches sustained him when he came to Corinth. That is why St. Paul told them, "I robbed other churches, taking wages from them in order to minister to you free of charge," and this seems to have been the usual custom. We read in Philippians 4:16 that the church at Philippi aided St. Paul more than once while he was preaching in Thessalonica, and the churches of Macedonia aided him when he was in Corinth. So he received support from other churches while preaching.

**11:9** **And when I was present with you, and in need, I was a burden to no one, for what I lacked the brethren who came from Macedonia supplied. And in everything I kept myself from being burdensome to you, and so I will keep myself.** One time, the support did not arrive on time yet he needed money. So, he did not have money coming from other churches while at the same time he did not charge Corinth, so what did he do? When his supplies fell short he worked as a tentmaker, as we read in Acts 18:3. He worked by his own hands as a tentmaker to support himself, until Silas and Timothy came from Macedonia with supplies. The word "brethren" in verse 9 is referring to Silas and Timothy. St. Paul was telling them, "Even when I needed money, I did not become a burden on any of you, but I worked with my own hands to support myself and waited until Silas and Timothy brought supplies from Macedonia. And in everything I kept myself from being burdensome to you, and so I will keep myself. I am determined to do the same and will not change. Even after the accusations I will not change, I will continue to preach the Gospel free of charge to you."

**11:10** **As the truth of Christ is in me, no one shall stop me from this boasting in the regions of Achaia.** He told them, "I am saying the truth in Christ, I am not lying. And no one, not even these false teachers, will be able to stop me from this boasting that I preached the Gospel free of charge to you in Achaia. So, as I have done, I will continue to do, and will boast in preaching the Gospel freely in Achaia."

**11:11   Why? Because I do not love you? God knows!** "They tell you that I did not take any money from you because I do not love you. Does this make sense to you? Only God knows the truth. God knows how much I love you." As he says in the following chapter, "When I love you more, you love me less." He was telling them, "Do I refuse to receive anything from you because I do not love you? I am not waiting for these false teachers to tell you whether I love you or not; God knows that this is not the case."

**11:12   But what I do, I will also continue to do, that I may cut off the opportunity from those who desire an opportunity to be regarded just as we are in the things of which they boast.** The false teachers took advantage of the Corinthians and burdened them with many, many financial and monetary demands. They were justifying this by saying it is because they were the apostles of Christ and that they love them, that is why they do not feel ashamed to take money from them. St. Paul knew that these false teachers were burdening them with their financial demands, that is why St. Paul insisted on not taking money—as a way of telling them that an apostle should not burden his children; a real father does not burden his children. If he had started to take money, he would be giving opportunity to the false teachers to continue taking

money from them and burdening them more and more with money. That is why he told them, "What I do I will also continue to do; I will continue not to receive any money from you, why? That I may cut off the opportunity, I do not want to give any opportunity to false teachers to say, 'St. Paul takes money, we also take money, so we are equal,' so I may cut off the opportunity from those—the false teachers—who desire an opportunity. They are waiting for an opportunity to be regarded just as we are, to say that as St. Paul receives money, we receive money from you."

**of which they boast.** They boast that they love them, that is why they receive money. But in reality, as St. Paul will explain in the following verse, they burdened them, they took advantage of them.

**11:13   For such are false apostles.** they consider themselves eminent apostles but in reality, they are false apostles.

**deceitful workers.** As Satan deceives people, his workers are also deceitful workers.

**transforming themselves into apostles of Christ.** Although they are false teachers, they come and tell you, "We are the apostles of Christ."

**11:14 And no wonder! For Satan himself transforms himself into an angel of light.** If Satan can take the form of an angel of light and deceives by coming in a false appearance, it is not that strange that his followers, workers, or servants will also present themselves as servants of righteousness—as the apostles of Christ.

**11:15 Therefore it is no great thing if his ministers also transform themselves into ministers of righteousness, whose end will be according to their works.** "His" refers to Satan—"Satan's ministers deceive you by presenting themselves as ministers of righteousness, but God will punish them according to their works, in the last day." ❖ And the most difficult thing or the surest wounds to the church, is not that which comes from inside but that which comes from the disciples of Satan, from within. For example, the persecution of Diocletian did not divide the Church, but Arius and Nestorius who were from inside and within the Church were able to divide the Church. We have to be very careful of those who are within but are false, those who claim to be ministers of Christ but are not preaching the truth; they pervert the Gospel of Christ and deceive many people by their deception. They present themselves like ministers of righteousness, but in reality, they are false apostles, deceitful workers. In the last day, at the second coming of Christ, they will be dealt with according to their works, not according to their pretense. They will be punished and their falsehood will be publicly revealed at the second coming of Christ.

**11:16 I say again, let no one think me a fool.** St. Paul started to reluctantly boast, knowing he should not do this, but he felt compelled. He knew it to be foolishness to boast and to commend oneself, and yet he felt compelled to do so in order to protect them. "I say again, let no one think me a fool. Do not think that I am a foolish person because I am boasting; I know very well that I should not boast, so please, do not think that I am a foolish person."

**If otherwise, at least receive me as a fool, that I also may boast a little.** Accept me as a foolish person, that I also may boast a little. If you accept me and say I am foolish, I will let this go. I will accept that you call me a foolish person in order that I may boast a little in order to defend your faith and present you as a chaste virgin to Christ. So even though I boast, let no one regard me as foolish because I am compelled by the criticism of the false teachers. But whether you regard me as foolish or wise, just listen to me, listen to what I am about to say.

**11:17** **What I speak, I speak not according to the Lord, but as it were, foolishly, in this confidence of boasting.** St. Paul is saying, "I know very well that the boasting I am about to do is not according to the Lord, is not consistent with Christian humility. Just listen to me, because the purpose of this boasting is to protect your faith. Why did St. Paul say that it is not according to the Lord? If St. Paul did not say this verse, then perhaps following generations will start to boast and take St. Paul as an example. This verse guards against his boasting being made a justification of boasting in general, so I would not come and boast before you about my achievement and say, "St. Paul did so." St. Paul was saying, "No, this is wrong, this is not according to the Lord, this is not consistent with the Christian virtue of humility, but I am compelled to do this for your own sake and because I am jealous for you with godly jealousy."

**11:18** **Seeing that many boast according to the flesh, I also will boast.** "According to the flesh" refers to heritage; we are the children of Abraham, we are from the chosen people of God, we have the Temple, we have the Law, we have the Ten Commandments. According to the flesh, boasting of external and secular things. St. Paul told them, "If they are boasting according to the flesh, I will also boast according to the flesh because

I am equal to them, I am not inferior to these false teachers in anything; I have the same privilege."

**11:19** **For you put up with fools gladly, since you yourselves are wise!.** Corinth is in Greece, which was known for philosophy and wisdom. As wise people, they took pride in that they put up gladly with foolish people. A wise person knows how to deal with foolish people. St. Paul, again in a tone of sarcasm, was telling them, "You put up with fools gladly because you are wise, so now listen to me. Even if I am foolish in your eyes, listen to me, put up with me, bear with me a little, because that is your pride, that you put up with fools gladly, you are so wise that you can bear with the foolish." Part of their wisdom was to tolerate the fools gladly.

**11:20** **For you put up with it if one brings you into bondage.** Here St. Paul explained how the false teachers took advantage of them. And he told them, "You did not only put up with the fools, but you allowed the false teachers to take advantage of you. If you allowed them to take advantage of you, just bear with me a little until I finish boasting. Even if you consider this foolishness, bear with me, listen to me because I want to deliver you from the deception of these false teachers."
❖   Christ has set us free from the

bondage of the Law, but they wanted to bring them back into the bondage of the Law.

**if one devours you.** The false teachers burdened them with financial demands, they devoured their property by their greed for gain, and they accepted this gladly.

**if one takes from you.** they took from them their belongings by craftiness and cunning snares.

**if one exalts himself.** they exalted themselves at your expense, they put you down in order to exalt themselves. How did they exalt themselves? When they claimed to be the "preeminent" apostles of Christ.

**if one strikes you on the face.** St. Paul was referring here to a serious abuse. They did not only devour them, lead them into bondage, took by cunning craftiness from them and exalted themselves at their expense, but they also physically abused them and slapped them on their faces. St. Paul told them, "If you accepted all this gladly and are defending them—these false teachers—again, put up with me, bear a little with me until I finish boasting."

**11:21** **To our shame I say that we were too weak for that!** One accusation that St. Paul referred to in the previous chapters is where they had said that in his letters, he is very strong and very bold, but when he comes and is present among you he is very weak; he does not discipline, he does not take any harsh action with you, so he is weak. That was their accusation against St. Paul. St. Paul responded to them saying, "To our shame I say that we were too weak for that! You perceived our genteelness as weakness because we did not abuse you like these false teachers. And you consider them strong because they abuse you, but we the gentle, you consider weak? And this became a shame, an accusation against us?

**But in whatever anyone is bold—I speak foolishly—I am bold also.** Now I will compare myself and you will see that I am also as bold as they are, but I cannot forget that this is foolishness; I speak foolishly. When I am bold or boasting, I cannot forget that it is foolishness to do this. In your eyes it is to our shame that we did not exercise power over you but were gentle. These false teachers accused that my presence was weak when instead I suffered among you; instead of exercising power over you, I suffered. But because they boast and are bold, I also boast and will explain to you in detail how I am equal, and maybe even better than these false teachers."

**11:22** **Are they Hebrews? So am I. Are they Israelites? So am I. Are they the seed of Abraham? So am I.** He initiated the physical boasting; the Judaizers were boasting that physically they are Hebrews, they are Israelites, they are the seed of Abraham, but St. Paul told them, "I am also a pure Hebrew, I am of the seed of Jacob so I am an Israelite, and I am heir to all the promises to Israel and also, I am not only from the fleshly seed of Abraham but also the spiritual seed of Abraham, because I have the faith of Abraham. So, when we speak about the physical boasting, I am equal, I am not inferior. Now let us come to my service as a minister of Christ."

**in stripes above measure.** In the next two verses (24 and 25), he will explain that five times he received forty strips minus one. Who else received stripes five times like St. Paul?

**in prisons more frequently.** St. Clement at the end of the first Century said in his letter to the Corinthians that St. Paul was imprisoned seven times. Only one imprisonment was mentioned in Acts 16:24, but there are six other imprisonments that we did not know about.

**in deaths often.** St. Paul was saying, "I was exposed to death, or suffering pain equal to death, or in danger of death several times."

**11:23** **Are they ministers of Christ?—I speak as a fool—I am more.** When he said, "I am more—I am better than them as ministers of Christ," again he said, "I speak as a fool, I should not say this but I will tell you, I will prove this by facts that I am not only a minister of Christ but I am a preeminent sufferer for Christ." To show how much he exceeded them, he gave accounts of his suffering. St. Paul repeated several times that it is foolishness to commend himself.

**in labors more abundant.** If you read the three missionary trips of St. Paul in the Book of Acts, you can know how St. Paul is more abundant than any other servant in his labors.

**11:24** **From the Jews five times I received forty stripes minus one.** According to the Law (Deuteronomy 25:3) the Jews were not allowed to exceed this number, so they used to stripe 39 times; they used this same number with the Lord Jesus Christ. St. Paul took the maximum number allowed by the Law—39. How many times? Five times. Five times he received 39 stripes.

**11:25** **Three times I was beaten with rods.** This was the Roman scourging and only one time was recorded in Acts 16:23, but there are two other times that were not mentioned in the Book of Acts..

**once I was stoned.** Acts 14:19 tells the story of the stoning of St. Paul

**three times I was shipwrecked.** when St. Paul wrote this letter there was no account given of these three times of shipwreck. Perhaps someone will say, "But there is an account in Acts 27 when he was travelling to Italy," but this shipwreck happened after he wrote that letter, so we can add this one, making them four not three times. If we add the one on the journey to Italy in Acts 27, then there are four that we know of, but there may be more.

**a night and a day I have been in the deep.** "The deep" means the depths of the water; either in an open boat or on a driftwood after a shipwreck. He spent a night and a day in water, in the depths of the waters—in the middle of the ocean or the middle of the sea after shipwreck.

**11:26 in journeys often.** St. Paul visited several countries and kingdoms to preach the Gospel, and we have the record of the three missionary trips in the Book of Acts. At that time there were no airplanes, there were no cars; there were not any of these methods of traveling or transportation that we currently use, yet St. Paul still travelled and visited many countries and many kingdoms to preach the Gospel.

**in perils of waters.** That is, with the threat of flooding, which made traveling very dangerous, perhaps he was in the middle of the sea or ocean and there was a storm or flood.

**in perils of robbers.** In his travels he was often exposed to the danger of attack by robbers and thieves.

**in perils of my own countrymen.** Referring to the Jews, who constantly persecuted him.

**in perils of the Gentiles.** The Romans also persecuted St. Paul. Here is suffering from the Gentiles who beat him with rods, and the Jews who many times persecuted and stoned him.

**in perils in the city.** "In the city" means while he was in the middle of the city, not in the desert, not in the wilderness. Here is just a partial record of how he was exposed to danger: in Damascus (Acts 9), in Jerusalem (Acts 21), in Antioch Pisidia (Acts 13), in Lystra (Acts 14), in Philippi (Acts 16), in Corinth (Acts 18). So, many times he was exposed to danger while he was in cities. be written.

**in perils in the wilderness.** While he was traveling he had to journey through the deserts and wilderness where he was exposed to dangers of robbers, wild beasts, hunger and thirst, wants, and sandstorms.

**in perils in the sea.** Like shipwrecks, like pirates, the ill-usage of mariners, the want of provisions while he was travelling at sea.

**in perils among false brethren.** False brethren like the false teachers, the Judaizers, who were always accusing him.

**11:27** St. Paul continues to list all the sufferings that he endured for Christ. All these verses show how St. Paul suffered self-denial, compromising his own body in order to preach the Gospel, suffering loss in order to preach Christ.

**in weariness and toil.** Often weary and in pain—of course exhausted—St. Paul was not young, he was old in age; he also had a disease in his eyes. He could not see well, that is why he needed someone to lead him, and also in writing, he needed somebody to write his letters. Thus, it was not easy for him, as he was weary and suffered from toil, and was in pain all the time.

**in sleeplessness often.** Perhaps he spent the night reading, preaching, praying, working by hand—he would preach in the morning at the Synagogue and at night work as a tentmaker in order to support himself.

**in hunger and thirst, in fastings often, in cold and nakedness.** hunger and thirst, involuntarily, like in the middle of the sea when they do not have provision, he has to go hungry and be thirsty. Fasting is actually voluntary—depriving himself of food maybe for prayer, or disciplining his body, or fasting for his people. He was often in want, hunger, thirst, nakedness and cold—surely during all these travels his clothes probably tore, so he had to travel in cold, and maybe he did not have enough clothes to cover himself, so he suffered from nakedness and cold.

**11:28** **besides the other things, what comes upon me daily: my deep concern for all the churches.** St. Paul was telling them, "Why did I endure all this suffering? Is it because I do not love you? Why did I endure all these perils? Because only conviction and love led me to this sacrifice, to accept all this suffering for Christ's sake and for your own sakes. This suffering and labor are not everything; you need to add to them my constant care for all the churches. All these physical sufferings and labors are not the only things that I suffer, besides the other things, what comes upon me daily. Every day comes with new responsibilities—my deep concern for all the churches. When I hear there is a problem in one church, there is division in another church, I feel torn from within and I do my best in order to help these people."

**11:29 Who is weak, and I am not weak?** I do not only care about the churches but I care about individuals. If I hear that someone is weak in faith I feel it is I who am weak, and I cannot have rest until I deliver him, I rescue him.

**Who is made to stumble, and I do not burn with indignation?** These false teachers who are putting stumbling blocks before you and causing you to stumble, cause me to burn from within with this Godly fire, with indignation, with this Godly anger. I sympathize with the churches and with the people, and if anyone suffers, I also suffer with him. If anyone is offended or stumbling, I actually feel the same pain, as if there is fire burning my heart from within.

**11:30 If I must boast, I will boast in the things which concern my infirmity.** St. Paul was saying, "I am sorry that I have said all these things. I should not boast in my achievements, I should not boast in my virtues, I should not boast in my endurance of all these sufferings; I should boast in my weakness rather than in my strength, that is why I will mention to you incidents in which I was weak and I could not endure for Christ.

**11:31 The God and Father of our Lord Jesus Christ, who is blessed forever, knows that I am not lying.** Perhaps someone will say, "Is it true that St. Paul really endured all this suffering? Maybe he is just lying, he is not saying the truth." St. Paul was taking God as a witness, because after giving this astonishing catalog of sufferings he said, "God knows that every word is true, I am not lying." ✤ And we need to learn this from St. Paul: wherever he mentions God he says, "Glory to Him, who is blessed forever," not like other Christians who say, "Jesus went, Jesus came."

**11:32 In Damascus the governor, under Aretas the king.** This story happened after St. Paul accepted Christ. You know that Christ appeared to him on the road to Damascus, so when he arrived in Damascus, the governor wanted to arrest him. St. Paul wanted to tell them, "From day one in Christ, I suffered."Aretas the king was the king of Petra and was also the father in law of Herod Antipas. Damascus was usually under Roman rule, but Aretas engaged in war with Herod because Herad had sent off his daughter and took Herodias for a wife. It may be that because of this Aretas made war with Herod and in defeating him became involved with the Romans; that may be why they added Damascus to be under his rule. In this war, Damascus fell under the hands of Aretas, and he appointed a governor.

**was guarding the city of the Damascenes with a garrison, desiring to arrest me.** There was a war at that time. This governor desired to arrest St. Paul because the Jews, who were very strong in Damascus, had asked the governor to try to cease St. Paul when they heard that he had become a Christian. St. Paul did not surrender himself, but escaped, and he considered this a weakness. That is why he told them, "You know what? I should boast in my weakness. I am telling you that I escaped, I did not allow the governor to arrest me. So, after I have mentioned to you the list of all these sufferings, I want to show you that I am also weak and that in this incident I actually escaped."

**11:33 but I was let down in a basket through a window in the wall, and escaped from his hands.** During St. Paul's time, they used to build houses against the wall of the city, and there were windows in this wall leading to the outside of the city. When the governor wanted to arrest St. Paul, they let him down in a basket through a window in the wall and he escaped from this governor. Maybe St. Paul did not find any other incidents of his weaknesses, that is why he only mentions this one incident of his weakness. He was so faithful, as he mentioned all his strengths, he also mentioned his weakness and said, "I know better, I should not boast in my strengths but I should boast in weakness." And actually, every time we read this chapter, words are short to express the greatness of St. Paul. All that he suffered, we as servants, feel embarrassed if we compare ourselves to St. Paul. What have we done as he did? There is no comparison, no one can say, "I suffered like St. Paul." ❈ When you feel tired or are persecuted, or there is pain or suffering in the service, go and read this chapter and you will know what suffering for Christ really means.

## Chapter 11 Questions

1. How did St. Paul desire to present the Corinthians to Christ?

2. What was St. Paul fearful of concerning the Corinthians?

3. What were they seemingly willing to put up with?

4. In what area did St. Paul concede that he was untrained? In what area was this not so?

5. What practice of St. Paul evidently was used as a charge against him?

6. Why would St. Paul continue the practice of not accepting support from the Corinthians?

7. While at Corinth, from whom did St. Paul receive support?

8. How does St. Paul describe these opponents of his?

9. How does Satan often transform himself? And his ministers?

10. How did St. Paul view the confidence of boasting?

11. Then why does St. Paul engage in such boasting?

12. In what three ways was St. Paul equal to his opponents?

13. List five things endured by St. Paul as a minister of Christ

14. If St. Paul must boast, in what would he boast?

15. What event does he relate as an example of his infirmity?

# 12

supernatural things with my spiritual eye.

**12:1 It is doubtless not profitable for me to boast.** St. Paul started by saying that without a doubt, it was not profitable for him to boast. And this is a teaching for us all, that it is not profitable to boast. Many people speak about their achievements and they boast about what they have done, but St. Paul told us, "Do not think it is profitable, it is without doubt unprofitable. But for me, I had to defend my apostleship and that is why even though I know this is foolishness, I was compelled to do so." St. Paul felt that it was distasteful to speak about himself but he was compelled because of the criticism of the false apostles and of his adversaries.

**I will come to visions and revelations of the Lord.** What is the difference between visions and revelations? Visions are the supernatural things revealed to the spiritual eyes. Revelations are the Divine truth revealed to the human spirit. So, when God reveals some truth, some Divine truth to my spirit, this is called revelation. A vision is when I see

**12:2 I know a man in Christ.** This man was St. Paul, but he felt it was not proper to speak about the visions and say that he was the man who was caught up to heaven. That is why when he spoke about the visions, he spoke in the third person. Also, from verse 7 in the same chapter we know that this "man in Christ" was St. Paul.

**who fourteen years ago.** if this letter was written in the year 57 A.D., then St. Paul was caught up to heaven in the year 43 A.D. 43 A.D. is about the time St. Paul was at Antioch with Barnabas, as we read in Acts 9:29-30, we can affirm that this vision did not happen during the time of his conversion because his conversion happened 20 years prior to the time of the writing of this epistle. Thus, we can say he was caught up to heaven six years after his conversion. Some people might say that perhaps this vision is the vision mentioned in Acts 22:17 when St. Paul was taken into a trance in the temple, but actually, the trance in the temple was many years after he was caught up to heaven. So, this event did not happen during the time of his conversion, neither is it the trance mentioned in Acts 22:17.

**whether in the body I do not know, or whether out of the body I do not know, God knows.** St. Paul is teaching us that a person caught up to heaven could see and hear without the body, hence, the human spirit is not material.

**such a one was caught up to the third heaven.** He said he was taken up to heaven, or "caught up to the third heaven," so what is the first heaven and what is the second heaven? The first heaven is the heaven of the birds, the air around us in which the birds fly. The second heaven is the space in which is the sun and all the stars, the galaxy. The third heaven is beyond the air, beyond the sun and the stars; it is called "Paradise." St. Paul did not speak in the first person; he did not say, "I was caught up to heaven," because it would be as if he was glorifying or glorying in his own exultation, and this is not proper. The word "Paradise" was mentioned three times in the New Testament. The first time was in Luke 23:43 when the Lord said to the thief on the Cross, "Today you will be with me in paradise." The second time is when St. Paul mentions it here, in second Corinthians 12, and the third time is when it is mentioned in Revelation 2:7 when the Lord said, "He who overcomes will eat from the tree of life, which is in the midst of the paradise of God." Paradise is the waiting place for the righteous until the second coming of Christ, so St. Paul was taken up to the heaven of the paradise.

**12:3 And I know such a man— whether in the body or out of the body I do not know, God knows.** He repeats again what he said previously: "Whether in the body or out of the body"—he did not know when he was caught up to heaven whether he ascended to heaven with his body or without his body.

**12:4 how he was caught up into Paradise.** St. Paul was saying that Paradise is the third heaven.

**and heard inexpressible words, which it is not lawful for a man to utter.** St. Paul heard words that were inexpressible, words that are not right to reveal in human speech. But he did not only say they were inexpressible, he said they were inexpressible words, which are "not lawful for a man to utter." It is as if God prohibited St. Paul from sharing these words with us. Thus, it was not possible because these words are inexpressible, and not right because it was not lawful for him to utter.

**12:5 Of such a one I will boast; yet of myself I will not boast, except in my infirmities.** "Of such a one I might glory, I might boast, but I will not glory as considers myself. When I speak about when I ascended to heaven, I will not speak as if it happened to me;

I will speak about it as if it happened to another person, a third person. But if I want to speak about myself, I will speak about my weaknesses and my infirmities."

**12:6 For though I might desire to boast, I will not be a fool; for I will speak the truth.** St. Paul was saying, "I am refraining from boasting about the visions directly, as if it had not happened to me directly, and why am I refraining? Is it because I am not saying the truth? No, I am actually saying the truth and I have the evidence that I am saying the truth. If I desire to boast about the visions I will actually not be a fool because I would be saying the truth. If I should boast of such a vision it would not be considered foolishness because I am telling you the naked truth.

**But I refrain, lest anyone should think of me above what he sees me to be or hears from me.** Why do I refrain and speak as if it happened to another person and not to me (regarding visiting Paradise, as noted in verses 3 and 4)? St. Paul answered this question by saying, "But I refrain, lest anyone should think of me above what he sees me to be or hears from me." St. Paul was saying, "On two different occasions people thought of me as God: when I healed the cripple person (in Acts 14:12–13) people thought of me as God, and when I shook off a viper from my hand, people thought of me as

God. So, what would they think of me if I disclosed these revelations and these visions as if they had happened to me?" "I do not want to mislead any person, I do not want any person to think of me as more than I am, more than he sees in me or more than he hears from me, because those who allow themselves to be thought of more highly, deprive themselves of their Godly honor" — as the Lord Jesus Christ told us in John 5:44 and John 12:43 — "So if I misled you to think of me more highly than I am, I am depriving myself of God's honor and God's glory."

**12:7 And lest I should be exalted above measure by the abundance of the revelations.** It is clear from this verse—"to be exalted above measure by the abundance of the revelations" –that the vision that he mentioned in verse 2 about being caught up to paradise, actually happened to him. And God wanted to keep St. Paul humble, that is why he allowed Satan to attack him with a physical disease.

**a thorn in the flesh was given to me.** A physical disease, a painful physical infirmity. Most scholars say it was a disease in his eyes, as he mentions in Galatians 4:13 and 14.

**a messenger of Satan to buffet me, lest I be exalted above measure.** All the physical evils are due to the sin and the fall of our forefather Adam and foremother Eve, and hence, all diseases are ascribed to Satan, that is why he said, "A messenger of Satan to buffet me." God was able to prevent it, but He did not prevent it because He used this disease in order to prevent undue exultation. God wanted St. Paul to be humble; He allowed this disease and this thorn in the flesh as a way to humble St. Paul.

**12:8** **Concerning this thing I pleaded with the Lord three times that it might depart from me.** St. Paul prayed three times that this disease may be removed. If it was a disease in his eyes, then it may have prevented him from traveling, may prevent him from reading, may prevent him from writing—that is why he prayed three times that God may remove this disease, in order to be able to read more, write more, travel more. His first and second prayers were not answered, or no answer came to St. Paul. That is why he prayed three times.

**12:9** **And He said to me, "My grace is sufficient for you, for My strength is made perfect in weakness." Therefore most gladly I will rather boast in my infirmities, that the power of Christ may rest upon me.** God answered him the third time. When we pray one time, two times, three times, and we do not

hear an answer, maybe God is waiting to give us an answer at the right time. And the answer to St. Paul was, "No, I will not heal you." ✤ Many times, we do not accept "no" as an answer. When we pray, for example, for the healing of someone dear to us and God does not heal them, we become angry and say, "Why does God not listen to my prayer?" However, St. Paul is teaching us today that God may answer our prayers by saying, "No." God will not always say "yes" to our prayers; He said "no" to St. Paul. God gave St. Paul the reason why He said no: "If you, Paul, are healthy, then you will serve relying and trusting in your physical abilities, but if you are weak physically, then you will serve trusting My grace. And My grace will be sufficient for you, My grace will provide you with the strength to travel, to write, and to read"—and he wrote more than half of the New Testament, he traveled between almost three continents, and he was reading until his martyrdom. God told him, "My grace is sufficient because when you realize that you are weak, you will allow My strength, or My power, to work to its fullest in you; My strength is made perfect in weakness. When you realize that you are weak, then My strength will work to its fullest, will be perfect in you." So the Lord answered his prayer not by removing his disease, but by giving him grace to bear it. By this assurance, St. Paul's sense of weakness—when he realized that he was weak because of the thorn in the flesh — fitted him to receiving the Divine strength. When you realize that you are weak, you will receive the Divine strength.

**12:10 Therefore I take pleasure in infirmities, in reproaches, in needs, in persecutions, in distresses, for Christ's sake. For when I am weak, then I am strong.** What was St. Paul's reaction? Was he angry because God did not heal him? Was he upset with God because God did not heal him? No, he said, "Therefore most gladly I will rather boast in my infirmities, that the power of Christ may rest upon me." He took pleasure in infirmities because the infirmities make him fit to enjoy the power of Christ. So, he said, "I am happy that I have these infirmities, I am happy that I have all these sufferings, because these sufferings and these infirmities qualify me to receive the power of Christ." It is when we feel our weakness that God strengthens us, because they bring us to a sense of our helplessness. When we feel that we are helpless, then God will actually make us strong.

**12:11 I have become a fool in boasting; you have compelled me. For I ought to have been commended by you; for in nothing was I behind the most eminent apostles.** After St. Paul finished boasting, when he looked back on what he had written, he found that he had done folly by boasting and by praising himself. Then he started rebuking the Corinthians telling them, "This ought not to have been done. I should not be boasting about my service or what happened to me, but you, the Corinthians, compelled me to boast because you did not commend me. If you had commended me and had accepted me as an apostle, I would not have had to boast." When he said, "You have every right to commend me for in nothing was I behind the most eminent apostles," St. Paul was referring to the false apostles, the false teachers who had claimed at Corinth to be leading apostles. As if St. Paul was saying, "In nothing was I behind those who claimed to be the most eminent apostles, though I am nothing."

**though I am nothing.** St. Paul is very, humble. He said, "I know that I am nothing and if anything in me is good, it is because of God, not because of me."

**12:12 Truly the signs of an apostle were accomplished among you with all perseverance.** While preaching in Corinth, he demonstrated his apostleship with all perseverance to those who opposed him, that is why he said, "with perseverance." He endured all the false apostles who opposed and attacked him, yet this did not cause him to leave his service. ✠ Many of us, when we find troubles in service, want to quit; but St. Paul, in spite of all these oppositions endured with perseverance. ✤ God sent the apostles with signs and miracles, and all the signs of the apostles were accomplished among you. And I want you to notice here that St. Paul did not say, "I accomplished among you," but he said, "Were accomplished," as if he was saying, "It is God who accomplished these signs in me. It is not I who accomplished these signs, but it is God who accomplished these signs through me." This is how he put himself as a worker in the background, by using the words "were accomplished" not the words "I accomplished."

**in signs and wonders and mighty deeds.** He was telling them, "You have enjoyed every privilege of the most highly favored churches—in wonders and mighty deeds and signs that happened in other churches, you have experienced the same."

**12:13** **For what is it in which you were inferior to other churches, except that I myself was not burdensome to you? Forgive me this wrong!** The one thing in which they differed from all the other churches was that St. Paul did not receive financial support from them, as he explained in the previous chapter. They complained that he had preached to them without charging them, and why did St. Paul do this? As he explained before, the false apostles were taking advantage of them in greed, so if St. Paul had taken

money from them, he would be giving opportunity to the false apostles to take more and more money from them in a greedy way. That is why St. Paul refused to take any money from them, in order to compel the false prophets not to receive any money from Corinth and thus, not take advantage of the Corinthians. But instead, the false apostles accused St. Paul of not loving the Corinthians and not trusting them, and that is why he did not receive any financial support from them. His accusers said that his declining support from them was a sign of lack of confidence and lack of love for them. St. Paul told them, "You are not inferior to any other church except in this one thing: I did not burden you with my expenses. And if this was wrong, I am asking your forgiveness." That is why he said, "Forgive me this wrong! If this was wrong, forgive me." But as he would explain, he insisted on doing this to edify them, to protect them, not because he did not love them, not because he did not trust them.

**12:14** **Now for the third time I am ready to come to you.** This saying means he visited them twice before. The first visit was when he founded the church, the second visit was while he was preaching in Ephesus, but this second visit was not mentioned in the Book of Acts.

**And I will not be burdensome to you.** "When I come again, as before, I will not be burdensome to you; I will maintain myself, I will support myself this third time." Why is that? St. Paul starts to make his argument that he did not receive any financial support from them, not because he did not love them, not because he did not trust them, but to actually protect them and to provide for them.

**for I do not seek yours, but you.** "I do not seek your money, but your salvation. The false apostles are after your money but I am after your salvation." ❖ This is a very important principle to us (the clergy and the servants) we should not be seeking yours, what you have, but we should be seeking you and your salvation.

**for I do not seek yours, but you. For the children ought not to lay up for the parents, but the parents for the children.** "Look at biological fathers: the children ought not to lay up for the parents but the parents lay up for the children. In the same way, as your spiritual father, I am laying up for you, I am not expecting you to support me. I, as your father, should support you. As biological parents do with their children, so I, your spiritual father, will do the same with you."

**12:15** **And I will very gladly spend and be spent for your souls; though the more abundantly I love you, the less I am loved.** St. Paul was

telling them, "I am not asking you to provide for me or to support me; I am giving you the Word of salvation, the Bread of life. And as a loving father I am glad to spend on you—to spend money on you, and I am also glad to be personally spent for you, to get tired, to persevere accusation, to persevere in persecution, to endure even death for your sake. As a father, I am willing to give up my life for your sake, although the more I love you the less I am loved by you." But this is the unconditional love of the servant—that without the return of his love he is willing to give more and more, to spend and be spent for them.

**12:16** **But be that as it may, I did not burden you. Nevertheless, being crafty, I caught you by cunning!** Some people accused St. Paul of craftiness: "St. Paul told you that he did not receive any money from you but this is not true, because he received money from you through his messengers. When he sent Timothy or when he sent Luke or when he sent Apollos, by sending these people, these people took money from you and gave it to St. Paul." St. Paul was refuting this accusation. He was telling them, "You may say that while I did not burden you myself, nevertheless, being crafty, I caught you in my net with cunning, I made gain of you by means of others, by using others to collect money from you." The false apostles accused St.

Paul of lying to them when he told them that he did not burden them, because by craftiness and cunning he took money from them by means of the messengers.

**12:17  Did I take advantage of you by any of those whom I sent to you?** St. Paul was asking them, "Did I make a profit off of you by any of the messengers or helpers I sent you? Did they demand anything? No, they did not demand any money from you."

**12:18  I urged Titus, and sent our brother with him. Did Titus take advantage of you? Did we not walk in the same spirit? Did we not walk in the same steps?** He said, "Yes, I sent Titus with the other brother" (2 Corinthians 8:18 and 22), perhaps Luke or Apollos. "Yes, I sent Titus and the other brother, but Titus and the other brother did not ask any money from you, did not take advantage of you. These accusers are lying to you because Titus and the other brethren walked in the same spirit" (that is inwardly), and the same steps (that is outwardly) "they followed my example both inwardly and outwardly. I did not use craftiness, I did not use any cunning to make gain off of you."

**12:19  Again, do you think that we excuse ourselves to you?** St. Paul is saying, "Do you think that we are defending ourselves before you, as before a human court? No, we speak before God in Christ. But we do all things, beloved, for your edification."

**We speak before God in Christ.** St. Paul was concerned lest any misunderstood him to be defending himself before them, so he told them, "No, I do not want to defend myself before any human being. I am only concerned about my words before Christ; I am speaking before God. So why am I defending myself? Not just to appear righteous before you, but rather I am defending myself and am explaining this for your edification. I did everything with this one goal— to edify you. My only objective is to build you up and not to clear my image before you."

**But we do all things, beloved, for your edification.** When St. Paul boasted, when he glorified himself, when he commended himself, when he defended himself, he did not do any of these things in order to clear his image; he did these with one main goal: "your edification"—"But we do all things, beloved, for your edification." He did everything in order to edify them; that was his only objective, to build them up.

**12:20  For I fear lest, when I come, I shall not find you such as I wish.** "I am trying to edify you, because I am concerned that when I come the third time I will not find you repentant, as I wish. If you have not repented by the time I come to you, I will discipline you severely, and you do not wish to see me in this way. That is why I am now trying to edify you, so that when I come to you I will not be compelled to discipline you harshly and you also will not see me as a harsh father disciplining his children." He feared that when he goes to Corinth he would have to rebuke severely on account of the sins he would find.

**lest there be contentions, jealousies, outbursts of wrath, selfish ambitions, backbitings, whisperings, conceits, tumults.** All these sins are sins of division that divide the church into parties. St. Paul was telling them, "I am concerned left when I come I find you divided against yourselves. If so, I will rebuke you severely because if you are divided against yourselves, you will give place to Satan. Any church or any kingdom that is divided against itself will be destroyed, and I do not want the church in Corinth to be destroyed." Contentions are like strife. Jealousies are like envy. Outbursts of wrath— wrath is destructive anger, when we yell and scream and abuse one another. Selfish ambition is actually self-seeking division, because when we are divided, everyone seeks his own interest. Backbiting is slandering openly, whispering is slandering in secret, conceits are the puffing up of yourself—to make yourself higher than you are—and tumults are like uproars, turmoil, and divisions amongst themselves.

**12:21  lest, when I come again, my God will humble me among you, and I shall mourn for many who have sinned before and have not repented of the uncleanness, fornication, and lewdness which they have practiced.** "I am also concerned lest some of you continue to live in the sins of the Gentiles without repentance." And he mentions three sins here: uncleanness—which is when married people commit adultery or have affairs, fornication—which is when unmarried people have affairs or commit adultery, and lewdness— which is when they commit sins against nature, like homosexuality. These sins were common amongst the Gentiles, that is why he was concerned lest they relapse and fall back into the same sins which he rebuked so severely in the first and second Letters to the Corinthians. ✶ God may permit to humble the priest, as he said, "I shall mourn" — by the fall of his people as if they were his own sins. When a priest or pastor sees his people struggling with sexual or sensual sins, this will humble him before God and make him mourn as if these sins were his own sins. St. Paul said, "Maybe God wants to humble me more—if I come and I find you struggling with these sins. But I want you to repent, and when I come to you, I do not want to see the married living in uncleanness or the single living in fornication or anyone among you living in a sin against nature; in lewdness."

## Chapter 12 Questions

1. Where was the "man in Christ" taken?

2. Of himself, in what would St. Paul boast? About what was he concerned?

3. Why was St. Paul given "a thorn in the flesh"?

4. How many times did St. Paul plead with the Lord to remove the "thorn"?

5. What did the Lord respond?

6. In what, then, did St. Paul choose to boast? Why?

7. What were the "signs of an apostle" that St. Paul had done among the Corinthians?

8. What had St. Paul done that some charged made the Corinthians inferior to other churches?

9. What was the motive behind all that St. Paul did for the Corinthians?

10. What was St. Paul afraid might occur when he got to Corinth?

11. What was St. Paul afraid of finding at Corinth?

# 13

## Chapter Outline

- Coming with Authority (1-6)
- St. Paul Prefers Gentleness (7-10)
- Greetings and Benediction (11-14)

**13:1** **This will be the third time I am coming to you. "By the mouth of two or three witnesses every word shall be established."** If you read the Book of Acts you will find that only two visits were recorded—one visit in Acts 18 and the other visit in Acts 20. This means there was an intermediate visit between these two visits, but it was not recorded in the Book of Acts. After he told them, "This is my third visit to you," he quotes a verse from Deuteronomy 19:15, "By the mouth of two or three witnesses every word shall be established." Different scholars have different interpretations of why St. Paul used this verse here. There are two explanations: Corinth had some false apostles and some offenders, so St. Paul was telling them, "This is my third visit to you and this time I am coming to discipline and to punish the offender, but when I discipline or punish them I will be very fair, I will use justice. And by the mouth of two or three witnesses, every word shall be established, so every offense will be disciplined but the trials will be legal;

two or three witnesses will establish a charge. Other scholars said, "By the mouth of two or three witnesses every word shall be established," he was referring to his two or three visits. He had already visited them twice and now this was the third visit. So it was as if he was telling them, "By this third visit I establish the truth of the fact alleged against the offender and I will establish the reality of my threats," because St. Paul threatened that when he went this time, he would not spare; that when he went this time he would punish, this time he would discipline. As if he was telling them, "If any word will be established by the mouth of two or three, now I endured you for three times, so the third time I will not spare, because now every offense has taken a fair chance and I gave them chance to repent but they did not repent. I am now coming to show you the truth of the facts about the accusations made by the offenders, the false apostles." I personally prefer the first explanation, that he is saying, "I will punish every offense and every trespass but the trial will be very fair and will be legal, any charge should be established by at least two or three witnesses."

**13:2** **I have told you before, and foretell as if I were present the second time, and now being absent I write to those who have sinned before.** St. Paul was telling them, "When I was visiting you during my second visit, I told you that I will not spare the offenders if they do not repent; I will punish them. Now I am putting it in writing, that when I come again, I will not spare the offenders." He was telling them, "As I told you before, when I visited you during my second visit and now while I am absent I am writing to you, that those who sinned before—those who sinned before my second visit, because during my second visit I told you this about those who sinned.

**and to all the rest, that if I come again I will not spare.** "The rest" refers to those who sinned after his second visit or those who are in danger of being offenders, "Now I am telling you, if I come again I will not spare, I will punish and I will discipline." But St. Paul understood that his punishment or discipline had a very clear goal, which is to edify, to lead them to repentance. When he disciplines, when he punishes, he is using his authority for edification and not for destruction.

in punishing, but St. Paul was kind and he chose to endure and have patience and longsuffering like the Lord Jesus Christ. But they accused him of not having proof of his authority, because if he had proof of his authority he would discipline and punish. St. Paul told them in verse 3, "Since you seek proof of Christ, you are seeking the evidence that I have authority, proof that I am an apostle. This proof is not weak toward you but mighty in you because it appeared in establishing the church, in preaching Christ to you, in all the miracles and all the wonders that I performed among you." "But all of this was not enough for you. You want me to use my apostolic authority to discipline and to punish and only then will you say that I am an apostle of Christ. Since some of you deny my apostleship, now I will give you the proof of Christ through me. This time when I come, I will not spare. Although long ago Christ has shown great proof of His power through me among you, but this was not enough for you, so now when I come, I will use my authority to discipline and to punish."

**13:3 since you seek a proof of Christ speaking in me, who is not weak toward you, but mighty in you.** One of the accusations against St. Paul was that in his letters he was strong, but when in their presence he was kind, he was weak. And when they compared St. Paul with the false apostles, the false apostles were strong in disciplining and

**13:4 For though He was crucified in weakness.** St. Paul was taking Jesus Christ as an example. They said that he was weak. He responded saying, "When the Lord Jesus Christ died on the Cross, many people perceived Him as weak, as you perceive me now as weak, but as Jesus Christ rose in power and might, the same power is working in me and working in every Christian."

**yet He lives by the power of God. For we also are weak in Him, but we shall live with Him by the power of God toward you.** Christ submitted Himself unto death by His own will, choosing the weakness of mortality when He chose to die, but by the power of God He rose from death on the third day. As Christ appeared weak, in the same way, we appear weak by accepting the same suffering of Christ—by partaking in this same suffering for His sake."

"As Christ rose, we also shall live with Him, and by the power of the resurrection of Christ, we will exercise our apostolic authority against the offenders. This power, this authority, flows to us with respect to you, from the power of God. God gave me this authority and empowered me to discipline and to punish the offenders among you."

**13:5 examine yourselves as to whether you are in the faith.** St. Paul wanted to give them two messages here. The first: I am coming to punish so it is better to examine yourselves. The second: "Instead of examining me and seeking proof of Christ in me, it would be better to examine yourselves. If you are eager to take the speck out of my eye, it would be better to remove the beam first from your own eye."

✤ We should all listen to this advice,

to examine ourselves in order to see whether we are in the faith, whether we are living the faith which we believe or not, whether we are abiding in Christ or not.

**Test yourselves. Do you not know yourselves, that Jesus Christ is in you?** "If Jesus is in you, then you would not be seeking proof that I am an apostle of Christ. If Jesus is in you then you would know that I am an apostle of Christ. If you find Christ dwelling in you, you will believe that He speaks also in me and I am His apostle."

**unless indeed you are disqualified.** "Christ should dwell in you, Christ must be in you, because through the sacraments of the church He told us, 'He who eats My body and drinks My blood abides in Me and I in him.' The only reason why Christ would not be in you is if you are disqualified, because of the sinful life in which you are living, because of the non-repentant status in which you are living."

**13:6 But I trust that you will know that we are not disqualified.** "If Christ is abiding in you, then you will know that I am not disqualified but that I have the apostolic authority— unless you yourselves are disqualified. Christ dwells in those who are qualified, those who do not reject Him, those who obey His commandments, those who are living by the power of the Spirit."

The power of Christ would show them that St. Paul was qualified, was an apostle of the Lord Jesus Christ. The power of Christ which St. Paul would display when he came on his third visit (by disciplining and punishing the offenders), would also show that St. Paul himself was not disqualified. This verse implies a threat: "When I come you will know for certain that I am not disqualified because I will not spare; I will punish the offenders. I will show you the proof that you are seeking during this visit."

**13:7–10**  After St. Paul said, "I will not spare, I will punish, I will discipline," from verses 7 to 10 he wanted to tell them, "But my heart, actually, does not agree with this. I prefer to use gentleness, I prefer to use kindness rather than disciplining and punishing." Let us think about it this way: if everyone in Corinth repented so that when St. Paul went there he would find everybody repentant, then he would not discipline anyone, he would not punish anyone. This would work against him because they want to see evidence of his authority only in punishing, but if everyone repented then St. Paul would not have the chance to show himself as powerful, as authoritative in the Lord Jesus Christ. St. Paul told them, "You know what, it is better for me that you perceive me as disqualified, that you perceive me as weak, that you perceive me as having

no authority and that you repent, than if you do not repent and I punish and prove to you my authority." This is the heart of a shepherd: he does not care about defending himself, he prefers and chooses to be accused as being weak and having no authority while everyone repents, rather than to defend himself and show his authority while the people fall in sin. These four verses are some of the most wonderful verses to show us the heart of St. Paul as a really good shepherd, following the footsteps of his Master. He prefers to appear as if he is disqualified or is weak, rather than to use his authority and appear as strong and powerful.

**13:7**  **Now I pray to God that you do no evil, not that we should appear approved, but that you should do what is honorable, though we may seem disqualified.** "I pray that you do no evil. I am not praying for an opportunity to show you that I have authority, rather I am praying that you do only what is honorable, even if the cost is that I would seem to you as if I am disqualified—I am fine with that." If they should do evil, St. Paul's display of power would show that he is not disqualified. But St. Paul said, "I do not pray that we be approved, I am not praying that you continue in evil so that when I come you would know that I am not disqualified, when I restrain you from doing evil, but I am actually praying for you to do only what is honorable. I am praying that you do no evil, but only what is right."

**13:8** **For we can do nothing against the truth, but for the truth.** If St. Paul went there and found everyone walking in the truth and repentant, he would not use his authority against these innocent or repentant people just to show them his authority. He told them, "I assure you that we do nothing against the truth, but only for the truth. Do not be afraid. Perhaps some of you are concerned that I will use my authority regardless, whether you repent or not; no, I only desire to promote the truth."

**13:9** **For we are glad when we are weak and you are strong. And this also we pray, that you may be made complete.** St. Paul told them, "If you are strong through your repentance, strong in your faith, strong because you carry the fruit of the Holy Spirit, and I am weak because I have no occasion to display the power of my apostolic authority, I am happy, I am glad, because I am praying for your complete restoration and transformation. I am praying that you will be made complete, perfect as your heavenly Father is perfect."

**13:10** **Therefore I write these things being absent, lest being present I should use sharpness, according to the authority which the Lord has given me for edification and not for destruction.** St. Paul was saying, "I am writing to you right now, before coming to visit you, to give you an opportunity to repent, because I prefer that when I come to visit you I would not need to use any sharpness. I prefer not to use any sharpness when I come, not to use authority or the power of God to discipline, although I understand this power is given for edification, not for destruction."

Here I want to speak just a little bit about authority. When God gives authority, either to a priest in a church, or a bishop in a diocese, or to a husband to be the head of a wife, or a parent in a family, or a manager in business, you should know that this authority is given to you to protect and to edify, not to abuse. This authority is given to you to serve others, not to be served by others. Unfortunately, many people do not understand this concept of authority—authority to edify, authority to protect. When we say that the husband is the head of the wife, this authority is to protect her, to edify her. Before he demands submission, a husband should provide protection, provide love, and thus, the submission will come as a natural fruit of this authority. St. Paul knew that even if he used sharpness to discipline, he would be using this sharpness only to edify, not to destroy; "But although I understand that I use sharpness to edify, not to destroy, I prefer to use sharpness only in my letters, and when I come, I prefer to use gentleness and kindness."

**13:11 Finally, brethren, farewell.** The word "farewell" in Greek also means "rejoice." In bidding farewell, he returns to his starting point. In the first chapter he told them, "We are fellow workers of your joy. He was concluding the letter by saying, "Rejoice. We are helping you to rejoice in the Lord and I say again, rejoice." Then he gave them four pieces of advice:

**Become complete.** (1) of 4. "Become complete," what does this mean? By filling up what is lacking in your Christian character. You should examine yourself and see what is lacking in your Christian character. Perhaps you are lacking humbleness, maybe you are lacking charity, maybe you are lacking gentleness, maybe you are lacking being a peacemaker, and you need to fulfill what is lacking in your Christian character.

**Be of good comfort.** (2) of 4. St. Paul was telling them, "If you listen to all my advice in this letter, you will have consolation in your hearts, you will be comforted. Obey the word of God, obey His commandment and be of good comfort." That is the only way to have comfort in your heart—when you obey the commandment of God.

**be of one mind.** (3) of 4. Corinth had

divisions, they were four parties. St. Paul was telling them, "No—think the same; let there be no dissensions among you."

**live in peace.** (4) of 4. Follow peace, pursue peace, be a peacemaker, try to reconcile people with each other, and you yourself should be a peacemaker.

**and the God of love and peace will be with you.** If you follow the four pieces of advice in this verse (noted above), what will be the fruit? The God of peace and love will be with you. But if you do not follow this advice and you are full of contention, dissention, discord, then peace will have no place among you. If you are divided against yourselves, peace and love will have no place among you, and if there is no peace and no love then God is not existing among this group. Love cannot live (neither exist) where there are divisions and contentions, and where there is no peace nor love, God cannot be there; the grace of God, the blessings of God cannot be there. If God is not there then who will be there? The devil, so their assembly will be an assembly of the people and the devil, not the people and God.

**13:12 Greet one another with a holy kiss.** He was giving them advice here on how to live in peace with one another, how to let the spirit of friendship live among you, how to reconcile with one another. He specified "holy kiss"; because a kiss can be used as an expression of lust or as an expression of deceit, just as Judas Iscariot betrayed the Lord Jesus Christ with a kiss. That is why he told them, "With a holy kiss"—not the kiss of the traitor and not the kiss of lust. ❖ The Coptic Church uses this greeting: "Greet one another with a holy kiss," in the Divine Liturgy. This was one of the Apostolic Canons mentioned in the Apostolic Constitution. In the Divine Liturgy in the Eucharist, we greet one another with a holy kiss as a sign of reconciliation, because if we are not reconciled with one another we cannot be reconciled with God. Only during Passion Week, from Wednesday to Saturday, do we not use the kiss of peace, in commemoration of Judas's kiss, which was a kiss of a traitor.

**13:13  All the saints greet you.** He is most probably referring to the Christians from Macedonia or Philippi, from where he wrote this epistle.

**13:14  The grace of the Lord Jesus Christ, and the love of God, and the communion of the Holy Spirit be with you all. Amen.** When St. Paul said "God," he was referring to the Father. This benediction proves the doctrine of the Triune God—that God is three hypostases in one; Trinity in unity. He spoke about the grace of the Son, the love of the Father, and the communion of the Holy Spirit. Usually when we mention the Trinity, we mention the Father, the Son, and the Holy Spirit, but St. Paul actually started with the Son, then the Father, then the Holy Spirit, because the Holy Trinity can be mentioned in any order because the Three are one. There is no supremacy in the Holy Trinity; thus, they can be mentioned in any order. ❖ As the three hypostases are inseparable, whoever has the fellowship of the Holy Spirit also has the grace of the Son and the love of the Father. And as the Holy Spirit is inseparable, so these three gifts cannot be separated in us, you cannot have one without the other. If you have the grace then you will come to know the love of the Father, and then you will enter into the communion of the Holy Spirit. So, whoever has the fellowship of the Spirit also has the grace of the Son and the love of the Father, because they are inseparable and the Holy Spirit is also inseparable

**grace of the Lord Jesus Christ and the love of God.** Why did St. Paul start with the grace of Christ? Because only by the grace of Christ do we come to know the love of the Father. Without the grace of Christ we would not know the love of the Father; the grace of Christ revealed to us how much the Father loved us, that is why he started with the grace of the Lord Jesus Christ and the love of the Father.

**communion of the Holy Spirit.**
Communion means fellowship of the
Holy Spirit, participation in the same
Spirit, who joins us all in one church.
Each one of us received the Holy Spirit,
and by all of us receiving the Holy Spirit,
we have become members in the body
of Christ. All of us are participating in
the same Spirit, the same Spirit dwells
in all of us, the same Spirit joins all of
us in one church; the body of Christ.

## Chapter 13 Questions

1. What will be the significance of St.
   Paul's third visit to them?

2. What is St. Paul's warning should
   he come again?

3. What does St. Paul exhort them to
   do?

4. What was St. Paul's prayer for them?

5. Why was St. Paul writing this
   epistle?

6. In expressing farewell, what four
   exhortations does he leave with
   them?

7. Provided they heed these four
   exhortations, what blessing will
   they enjoy?

8. What final exhortation does he give
   to them?

9. What three blessings does St. Paul
   pray for them as he closes this
   epistle?